03527

973.75
H

Horner, Dave
    The blockade-runners; true tales of running the Yankee blockade of the Confederate coast. Illus. with photos. Drawing by Jack Woodson.   Dodd [1968]
    241 p. illus.

    Includes bibliography.

    1. U.S.--Hist.--Civil War--Blockade.

NPLC99

THE BLOCKADE-RUNNERS

Also by Dave Horner

Shipwrecks, Skin Divers, and Sunken Gold

Better Scuba Diving for Boys

973.75
H

THE BLOCKADE-RUNNERS

*True Tales of Running the Yankee Blockade
of the Confederate Coast*

By DAVE HORNER

Illustrated with photographs
DRAWING BY JACK WOODSON

DODD, MEAD & COMPANY, NEW YORK

*This Book Is Dedicated Affectionately
to My Wife, Jayne*

Acknowledgments

The author gratefully acknowledges those who willingly offered a helping hand with this book. Special mention goes to Hall Watters of Wilmington, North Carolina, a fish-spotter pilot and scuba diver *extraordinaire*, who knows more about sunken blockade-runners than ol' Davy Jones, himself. To Charles H. Foard, "noted historian of the lower Cape Fear," who has spent a lifetime researching the blockade-running era and who always was able to come up with the answer to a difficult question, I extend sincere appreciation. I am indebted also to my good friend Jim Wamsley of Richmond, Virginia, editor of *The Commonwealth* magazine, who generously assisted in some of the difficult research and shared in the writing of several chapters.

In Bermuda, Terry Tucker was most helpful at the Bermuda Library and Museum, and Charles Pearman-Wilson, associate editor of *The Bermudian* magazine, graciously permitted use of material from his publication; Harry Cox managed to leave his cabbage and cucumbers and crank up the *Shearwater* long enough to get us to the outer reefs, although the old Spanish shipwrecks in the vicinity did cause my interests to stray from blockade-runners; and

Teddy Tucker offered sound advice and shared some of his experience on the Bermuda reefs.

It is a privilege to thank Miss Virginia Rugheimer of the Charleston Library Society, Mrs. G. T. Prior of the South Carolina Historical Society, and Mrs. Roberta Bonnoit of the Charleston County Library, all of whom helped provide original source material in Charleston, South Carolina.

The usual interest and able assistance of Milton C. Russell, Head Reference Librarian of the Virginia State Library, and Mrs. Willie Anna Jarrall is greatly appreciated.

I should also like to recognize Stanley A. South, Archaeologist, North Carolina Department of Archives and History; Ernest S. Dodge, Director of the Peabody Museum and Managing Editor of *The American Neptune*; John L. Lochhead, Librarian of The Mariners Museum; Elmer O. Parker of the National Archives and Records Service; Marcus W. Price; and Jack Woodson.

Other organizations and institutions that made contributions are Lloyd's of London; the Wilmington, North Carolina, Public Library; the Nassau Development Board; Library of Congress; the Lynchburg, Virginia, Public Library; and Maritime Explorations, Ltd., Virginia Beach, Virginia.

My thanks go, finally, to Virginia Gillispie, Ruby Deboe, Jean Moore, and Betty McCarthy, who helped with the endless typing; to Katherine Byers Horner, who came through as usual when there was editing to be done; and to Valerie, Vicki, and Julie, who did their best to entice me from the uncompleted manuscript.

Preface

At the time of the original blockade-running research for my book *Shipwrecks, Skin Divers, and Sunken Gold* I scarcely realized the magnitude of the topic.

During this early period of data gathering and wreck exploration I contemplated writing a relatively short book on sunken blockade-runners, listing their wreck sites, circumstances of sinking, cargo manifests, and so forth. But as I gradually became captivated by the subject, the more I realized the tremendous value of its contribution to the Confederate cause. Certainly the true story of Confederate blockade-running has hardly been told.

Few authors have gone to the trouble to review at great length the innumerable official dispatches of the Union and Confederate Navies. Furthermore, most sea operations of the Civil War received little publicity in view of widespread land battles and terrible casualties being suffered on both sides. By its very nature, blockade-running was highly concealed, and few of its mysteries were exposed.

My devotion to the study of American history, particularly the Civil War era, is natural enough. My great-grandfather, David Buffington Horner, was with General Lee to the very end at Appomattox; another great-grandfather,

Alexander Benjamin Mahood, was a paymaster in the Confederate government who had instructions to bury the Treasury gold when Richmond was evacuated; and still another great-grandfather, Samuel Byers, served as an aide to the famed General Ashby in the Shenandoah Valley.

Spurred on by my own personal interest in the blockade-running chapter of Civil War history, together with the qualified recommendations of my efficacious editor, Allen Klots, Jr., I decided to delve into this elusive subject more thoroughly. In addition to my personal knowledge as a diver on sunken blockade-runner wrecks, I worked also from original sources in the archives and references that have been long out of print. I visited many of the locations about which I was writing and, during such trips, made several valued acquaintances and some startling discoveries.

Excavating among previously unsalvaged wrecks of forgotten blockade-runners, as well as exploring original documents in libraries of Bermuda, Nassau, and the United States, I accumulated a wealth of information. Most exciting was the discovery of a corroded artifact in the hulk of a 100-year-old shipwreck, or a revealing phrase in a battered and musty manuscript. All of this has provided evidence to help me understand and relive the days of daring and adventure to which some historians have referred, but which few have portrayed with authentic documentation.

There is no doubt that blockade-running achievements made vital contributions to the Confederate war effort. It was this single factor which determined for the Southern States whether there would, or would not, be a successful conflict.

The accounts that follow are, to the best of my knowledge, a true saga of the exploits of Confederate blockade-runners, narrated as the story has never been told before.

—DAVE HORNER

Contents

Illustrations

I

THE YANKEES
ARE COMING

CHAPTER 1

Blockade-Running as a Business —
Causes, Conflicts, Cargoes, Conquests

It is not the purpose of this book to discuss the War Between the States or the unhappy causes leading to it. Many authors have covered this eventful subject most admirably. Both the Southern and Northern views have been treated in detail and their arguments submitted to impartial history. Now that the mists of prejudice and passion have cleared away, all Southerners agree that secession from the Union was impracticable. The Southern people have fully accepted the results of the terrible war. And today it is no secret that the South outpaces the North in many areas of growth and economic development.

The record of Southern courage that relates the story of a dedicated people who fought so long against insurmountable odds will always be a significant and memorable page in American history. Today those who look back on the mighty contest cannot help but be amazed at how the Southern States held out so long. As they defended their homeland against an enemy outnumbering them four to one in arsenals, machine shops, and an organized army and navy, we reflect in wonder how the South managed to win almost as many single victories as were won by the North.

The lost cause of the South was determined as much by its economic conditions and its never-to-be-achieved financial policies as by the long-range incapability of its military objectives. Since the North was much more industrially advanced, its army and navy organized, and its transportation and trade system better developed, there was never a question as to its ultimate victory. Blockade-running was only a temporary means by which the South prolonged the agony of facing the decision of defeat.

It is unfortunate, in retrospect, that the Confederate administration lacked a comprehensive plan of control over transportation. Practically everything necessary to conduct a war had to be brought into the country. Had there been prudent and long-sighted planning, the supply of food and arms and the transporting of troops need not have been as serious a problem. While Lee's famished soldiers in Virginia were on quarter rations and, at times, had no food at all, tons of provisions lay rotting at various railroad depots. Between Charlotte and Weldon, North Carolina, and Danville, Virginia, more than four months of rations for 60,000 men intended for General Lee were lost to him because of the inadequacy of the Confederate railroads.

Little wonder that in the days of 1861 the South, with an army of hardly 600,000 men and no navy, except for a handful of river steamboats and privateers, faced towering opposition. Northern armies outnumbered those of the Confederacy by more than 2,000,000 men. The Union Navy, experienced only in peacetime operations and unready at the beginning, was to become the nemesis of the South, unable to defend its coastline. Union sea power rapidly increased in force until it boasted some 700 warships manned by more than 105,000 sailors.

Most Southerners expected England and European countries with whom they engaged in trade to recognize the Confederate States of America as an independent government. They contended that the many cotton mills in Great Britain and France had no choice but to favor continued commerce with the Southern States and aid the Southern cause. At the same time it was apparent to Southern leaders that only by exporting cotton could they acquire the unlimited variety of supplies needed to fight a war. The Southern economy was primarily agricultural. It had neither the machinery, skilled labor, nor raw materials to construct the implements of war. There was hardly a nail factory in the entire Confederacy, and the few machine shops in business were very limited in production.

The only answer was to import supplies from abroad. But just a few days after the fall of Fort Sumter, Abraham Lincoln issued a proclamation declaring the blockade of the southern states between Virginia and Texas. An unavoidable result of this decree was blockade-running by individuals as well as by the Confederate government. Companies were formed and funds were raised by selling shares of stock to patriotic citizens who were as interested in realizing a quick profit as they were in supporting the Rebel cause for independence.

Blockade-running from Europe was attempted at the beginning, but the profits were not sufficient to justify the risks of the long transatlantic voyage. A plan of transshipment was then devised with larger and slower vessels to bring stores across the ocean to the intermediate points of Bermuda or Nassau. From there small, fast runners took aboard the cargo and made the short, illegal trip to the blockaded coast. In return for the stream of supplies that poured into the Southern States via the blockade-runners, the South made regular remittances in cotton to England.

A large amount of capital was invested in the new industry. Since the Confederate government was engaged in

blockade-running, agents were sent to England to arrange
for specially built vessels as well as the purchase of munitions and supplies. The Confederate States of America se-
cured four such vessels and was part owner in several others.
Colonel Josiah Gorgas was Officer in Charge of Confederate Ordnance. He supervised the running of vessels owned
by the Confederate government. These included the *R. E.
Lee*, *Merrimac*, *Phantom*, and *Cornubia*.

Among the wholly owned blockade-runners was the
Giraffe, later named the *R. E. Lee*, a Clyde-built iron side-
wheel steamer, of light draft and good speed. She formerly
had been used as a packet ship between Glasgow and Bel-
fast. Under her new name she was to become famous. Captain John Wilkinson, an officer of the U.S. Navy who
resigned to serve on the side of the South, was placed in
command. Under his able direction the *R. E. Lee* made
twenty-one successful runs in the ten months between December 1862 and November 1863 and carried abroad more
than 6000 bales of cotton worth about $2,000,000 in gold.

Usually the cotton was landed in Nassau, but the Confederate government did not appear on the invoices as shipper-
owner. This vital commodity was entrusted to large jobbing
houses which received very high commissions for assuming
ownership.

The mercantile house, or agents, that handled a blockade-
running company's business usually held a portion of the
stock. The commissions earned were of such extent that
even if individual stockholders lost money, the mercantile
house made handsome profits.

Although England never agreed to assist the South, many
of her native sons invested sizable sums in vessels designed
expressly for running the blockade. The United States Consul at Liverpool reported that "Members of Parliament,
mayors, magistrates, aldermen, merchants, and gentlemen,
are all daily violating the laws of nations." In 1864 he wrote,

"Nine-tenths of all vessels now engaged in the business were built and fitted out in England by Englishmen and with English capital, and are now owned by Englishmen."

Cotton was selling in England at fifty-five cents a pound. It could be shipped from Charleston at five cents per pound. With such profits involved, British speculators were willing to take anticipated risks! Confederate agents worked "hand-in-pocket" with the profit-seeking Britishers. Blockade-runners were manned by entire crews of English and European sailors interspersed with Confederate officers, secret agents, and coast pilots. One minute the British ensign flew, the next the Rebel Stars and Bars. Ships engaged in the contraband trade changed their names as often as their flags, and most of their skippers flaunted fancy aliases.

In the early days of the war the so-called Federal blockade was hardly more than wishful thinking. The Union Navy had only a handful of ships ready for action, and their officers were totally unfamiliar with this type of duty. The Federals, themselves, admitted they were hardly qualified to blockade 3500 miles of Rebel shoreline—a coast with numerous bays and inlets, a region of shifting sands and treacherous shoals, a land where supply bases would be restricted if at all possible to establish. Rear Admiral S. F. Du-Pont wrote Secretary of the Navy Gideon Welles in August 1862, off Charleston, South Carolina, "I am fairly oppressed by the insufficiency of the blockade. . . . I think it probable that some two million sterling of arms and merchandise have gone in the last ten days. . . ."

Union vessels, themselves, differed little from the century before. Large, lumbering, two and three deckers were similar in construction, rigging, and armament to the ships of Lord Cornwallis when England tried to repulse the first American claim for independence.

The use of steam in place of sail, however, was beginning to reveal many new developments to the seafaring trade.

Side-wheelers outclassed screw propellers, and iron out-matched wooden hulls. Oceangoing sloops-of-war of about 1000 tons and armed with a handful of 32-pounders were constructed expressly for chasing blockade-runners. Shallow draft 500-ton gunboats, capable of a speed of 10 knots were equipped with an 11-inch pivot gun and several 24-pound howitzers for patrolling Confederate rivers and bays. In the meantime, ferryboats, tugs, barges, and worm-eaten whaling vessels were converted to transports and ships of war by the Union Navy.

While the Northern Navy organized, the blockade-running business was beginning to become an extremely lucrative trade. In the early stages of the war all types of vessels had a try at "makin' a run." Worm-riddled sailing scows, schooners, and sloops of questionable origin all ran the blockade. Few had difficulty in slipping by the fumbling defensive line of Union warships. According to the *New York Sun*, $10 invested in quinine in Nassau would bring from $400 to $600 in Charleston.

As Yankee proficiency, speed, and sea power tightened, the slower sailing ships were captured and others who might have tried "jus' one more run" were deterred from doing so by the chance of being overtaken and destroyed. So, in the latter months of the war the story changed. More gunboats were made available, and efforts by Union blockaders reduced considerably the volume of cargoes being brought into or taken out of the South.

The blockade of Southern ports was to prove that it, alone, would be the most effective weapon of the North. The threat of being fired upon and killed or captured by a fast and heavily armed man-of-war called the bluff of many anxious, cargo-carrying, blockade-running skippers. Ordinarily they would have been more than willing to deliver supplies to the impoverished South.

Not only did the Union Navy build and put into service

an increasing number of fast gunboats, they also converted and utilized most of the blockade-runners they captured. These fast, maneuverable vessels were especially useful in chasing down other blockade-runners, and under the command of Yankee captains, many were highly successful at the game.

One renowned runner, captured after eighteen enormously profitable trips and condemmed as a prize, was the *Margaret and Jessie*. She was armed and renamed the *Gettysburg* and, with her new Yankee crew, was successful in landing the *Little Ada* bound for Charleston. She also captured the prize steamer *Lillian* and the brand new blockade-runner *Armstrong* bound from Wilmington to Nassau with 600 bales of cotton.

Since some blockade-runners were captured and converted for use by the blockading fleet in patrolling the coast, it was not an uncommon trick for a blockade-running captain, upon falling in with the Yankee fleet, to pretend that he was on similar duty. On one particular occasion, the notorious Captain John Wilkinson of the Confederate States Navy reported that "we shaped our course for Beaufort and, slowing down, . . . we passed several vessels, showing United States colors to them all. Just as we were crossing through the ripple of shallow water off the tail of the shoals, we dipped our colors to a sloop-of-war which passed three or four miles to the south of us. The courtesy was promptly responded to, but I have no doubt her captain thought me a lubberly and careless seaman to shave the shoals so closely."

Major problems to investors in this business were not only the increased number of blockading gunboats that were pressed into service by the North, but the continuing devaluation of Confederate currency.

The Confederates were paying English importers and jobbers tremendous prices for their goods. But on top of the high purchase price for supplies and merchandise, the figures were multiplied enormously when the items reached the Confederate States. Much of the difficulty lay in the fact that the price for cotton was not being increased in the same proportion. And this great difference in value between imports and exports resulted in improper balance of payments.

At the end of 1863 a dollar in gold was worth about $20.00 in Confederate Notes. In October, 1864, the Secretary of the Confederate Treasury stated, "Unless a uniform and stable value can be given to the Treasury Notes, the effort to carry on the war through their instrumentality must, of necessity, be abandoned." He further stated that $135.00 in Confederate currency was worth only $6.00 in gold, or about $22.50 in currency for each dollar in specie. By February 1865, one dollar in gold was equivalent to approximately $58.00 in Confederate Treasury Notes.

If the housewives of today think they have problems keeping within their food budgets, they should be in perfect position to sympathize with the women of the South in the early eighteen-sixties. According to J. B. Jones in *A Rebel War Clerk's Diary*, the following prices prevailed in 1863 as compared with 1860:

1860		1863	
Bacon, 10 lbs. @ 12½¢...	$ 1.25	Bacon, 10 lbs. @ 1.00...	$10.00
Flour, 30 lbs. @ 5¢...	1.50	Flour, 30 lbs. @ 12½¢...	3.75
Sugar, 5 lbs. @ 8¢...	.40	Sugar, 5 lbs. @ 1.15...	5.75
Coffee, 4 lbs. @ 12½¢...	.50	Coffee, 4 lbs. @ 5.00...	20.00
Tea (green) ½ lb. @ 1.00...	.50	Tea (green) ½ lb. @ 16.00...	8.00
Butter, 3 lbs. @ 25¢...	.75	Butter, 3 lbs. @ 1.75...	5.25
Candles, 2 lbs. @ 15¢...	.30	Candles, 2 lbs. @ 1.25...	2.50
Soap, 5 lbs. @ 10¢...	.50	Soap, 5 lbs. @ 1.10...	5.50
Pepper and salt		Pepper and salt	
(approximately)...	.10	(approximately)...	2.50

Not only were foodstuffs extremely scarce, but medicine, drugs, and surgical instruments had to be almost totally imported and brought tremendous prices once they reached the Confederacy.

The first blockade-running company to ship cotton from Charleston and import war materials was John Fraser and Company of South Carolina. This firm later became one of the largest and most active blockade-running businesses in the South. Its principal member, George A. Trenholm, was a highly successful businessman who later was named Secretary of the Treasury of the Confederate States of America. He was relied upon very heavily by the Confederate government and supported the war effort quite loyally by carrying as much freight as possible "consigned to the Confederate States of America." On numerous occasions John Fraser and Company were referred to as "bankers of the Confederacy."

Another well-known blockade-running company was the Importing and Exporting Company of South Carolina, commonly referred to as the Bee Company, because of its highly respected president, William C. Bee. It would be difficult, if at all possible, to state the number of bales of cotton this firm hauled to Nassau and Bermuda in exchange for munitions of war on the return voyage. A great number of battles were fought principally with the guns and ammunition, the shoes, food, and clothing brought into Southern ports by the Bee Company.

This blockade-running company probably did more for the Southern cause, irrespective of the motive for profit, than any other single organization. In December 1863 *The Charleston Daily Courier* announced that the Bee Company would endeavor to place imported merchandise at private sale rather than at auction where it was not unusual for expenses to get far out of hand because of the fantastic bidding by the retail merchants.

At an auction sale of the Importing and Exporting Company in Charleston, South Carolina, a pound of crushed sugar brought $4.00. It later sold in Richmond at $11.00 per pound.*

Not all shareholders of most individually owned block-ade-running companies made such money. But most of the principals, agents, and those who ran the blockade did. Many vessels were captured or destroyed, and wages paid were absurdly high. Devaluation of the Confederate dollar and the related consequences of high prices became an in-creasingly significant problem. In the Cotton and Captured Property Records at the National Archives, William C. Bee, himself, is on record stating that it "was a popular error that large profits were realized by the stockholders for the op-eration of the Company." He went on to further state that the cost of doing business was unbelievably high and that speculators should think first of the Confederate cause rather than their own personal gain.

The Charleston Mercury, however, reported on Decem-ber 28, 1863, the first dividend of the Bee Company at $5000 per share. *The Charleston Daily Courier* reported another dividend of $2000 per share in August 1864. In January 1865, a dividend was reported at $2000 in Confed-erate currency plus an additional 50 pounds sterling. Other dividends were paid in addition to these.

The Charleston Mercury of November 16, 1864, further illustrated the profits of blockade-running in reporting divi-dends of two other companies engaged in the business. The Anglo-Confederate Trading Company paid two dividends of $1000 and $1500 on its $100 par value stock in 1864. Also that year the Palmetto Importing and Exporting Company of South Carolina paid a $2000 dividend per share.

According to Marcus W. Price, "In 1863, 84 percent of all known attempts to penetrate the blockade of the Caro-lina ports were successful, and this figure decreased only

* From a William C. Bee letter published in *The Charleston Daily Cou-rier* on April 7, 1864.

1 percent in 1864. The percentage for both years would have been appreciably higher had it not been for the large number of unsuccessful attempts made by sailing ships." *

Thus, the magnitude of blockade-running and its measure of success are matters of historical record believed to be reasonably accurate. At the end of the war, Union records showed 1149 blockade runners captured, 210 being steamers. Even more noteworthy is the fact that 355 blockade-runners were sunk, burned, beached, or destroyed. Of these, 85 were steamers. The value of these vessels and cargoes was conservatively estimated at $35,000,000.

Records do not exist which might help determine the amount and value of arms, supplies, and merchandise that were brought into the Confederate States during the four years of blockade-running. However, a special report from the Confederate Secretary of the Treasury stated that the following stores had been imported at the ports of Wilmington and Charleston between the period of October 26, 1864 to December 6, 1864: ". . . 3,632,000 pounds of meat, 1,507,000 pounds of lead, 1,933,000 pounds of saltpeter, 456,000 pairs of shoes, 316,000 blankets, 542,000 pounds of coffee, 69,000 rifles, 97 packages of revolvers, 2,639 packages of medicines, 43 cannon, with a very large quantity of other articles."

The report further recorded that "from March 1, 1864, to January 1, 1865, the value of the shipments of cotton on Confederate government account was shown to have been $5,296,000 in specie, of which $1,500,000 had been shipped out between July 1 and December 1, 1864."

During the period September 30, 1862, to September 30, 1863, official records reflect that more than 113,000 small arms had been brought to Confederate ports via blockade

---

* From *Blockade-Running as a Business in South Carolina During the War Between the States, 1861–1865*, by Marcus W. Price, and appearing in *The American Neptune* magazine, January, 1949, Salem, Massachusetts.

runners as well as tremendous quantities of cartridges, percussion caps, lead, saltpeter, and general hardware. From December 1, 1863, to December 1, 1864, some 500,000 pairs of shoes were imported, together with about 300,000 blankets. During this same period, some 8,000,000 pounds of meat and 500,000 pounds of coffee were reportedly brought through the blockade.

Albert Sidney Johnston's army fought the battle of Shiloh with Enfield rifles brought in by the blockade-runner *Fingal* (afterward known as the *Atlanta*) on November 12, 1861. Her cargo included 1,000,000 ball cartridges, 2,000,-000 percussion caps, 10,000 Enfield rifles, 3,000 cavalry sabers, 1,000 short rifles and cutlass bayonets, 1,000 rounds of ammunition per rifle, 500 revolvers and ammunition, two large rifled cannon and firing equipment, 400 barrels of cannon powder, and assorted medicines and clothing.

Sneaking through the Yankee fleet was considered "easy" by some blockade-running skippers. In the words of John Wilkinson, "Although the blockade-runner might receive a shot or two, she was rarely disabled; and in proportion to the increase of the fleet, the greater would be the danger (we knew) of their firing into each other. As the boys before the deluge used to say, 'They would be very apt to miss the cow and kill the calf.' "

Besides the cordon of vessels on blockade duty around Wilmington, Charleston, and the major Gulf ports, the fast oceangoing Yankee cruisers patrolling the Gulf Stream on the courses between Bermuda and Nassau were highly effective in spotting the runners. In fact, with the advent of the new, fast cruisers most blockade-runners feared the open sea to a greater degree than harbor entrances or an unknown shoal. The cruisers, upon discovering a lead-colored, suspicious-looking intruder, would send up a dense column of black smoke notifying sister ships in the area. If the trap worked, several blockaders would close in on the runner from various directions.

For the most part it was a cat-and-mouse, fox-and-hound, hide-and-seek game. The blockade-runners were able to set the pace and call the plays, for they usually were in the best position. They could select the time, place, and other conditions which, more often than not, included a moonless night and a rising tide. All of these factors would increase their odds of maneuvering over the shoals as they raced for a Confederate port.

Having outdistanced or bypassed the outside blockade, the blockade-runner would lie offshore of her destination waiting for darkness and the tide. When harbor entrances were active with cruisers, nearby inlets would serve as proper shelter. The runner would blend in perfectly with the shadows of the sand dunes in the background. At the right moment, the fugitive vessel would move out of hiding, hugging the shore in order to slip by the blockading line of gunboats.

Sometimes they were spotted by the blockading fleet and cut off before they could reach their destinations. Under such circumstances it was common practice for the captain to run his vessel ashore, hoping to beach a portion of the cargo before being captured.

Nassau and Bermuda were the most prominent neutral ports and provided intermediate harbors for hauling contraband in exchange for cotton. Nassau was only about 560 miles from Charleston, and Bermuda was about 674 miles, a three-day run, from Wilmington.

For the passage between the neutral islands and the Rebel shore, speed was essential. The popular blockade-runner of 1863–1864 was a slender, low, side-wheel steamer of about 500 tons. Its length was usually nine times its beam. The runners often were referred to as Clyde steamers, since many were constructed on the Clyde River in Scotland. The hull was painted either a lead gray color or a light cloudlike color which could hardly be seen in daylight at a few hundred yards. Anthracite coal, which made no smoke, was the most desirable fuel.

Special precautions were taken to keep from being seen, especially at night, when they were near Yankee warships. No lights were allowed, nor was any smoking. The engine room hatches were covered with tarpaulins "at the risk of suffocating the unfortunate engineers and stokers in the almost insufferable atmosphere below." Even the binnacle was covered, with only a small peephole through which to see the compass.

Most blockade-running captains were able to pick their own crews, for men were ready and willing since compensation was at a premium. The British Navy found it difficult to keep their crews from deserting because of the great temptation of running the blockade.

For a single trip from Nassau to Wilmington and return, the pay rates were as follows in pounds sterling:

Captain	1000
Pilot	750
Chief Engineer	500
Chief Officer	250
Second and Third Officer	150
Crew and Firemen	50

Half the money was offered as an inducement at the beginning of the voyage, and half rested upon the successful completion of the trip. It was reported that many blockade-running captains could afford to retire after six successful months in the trade.

Not only did those aboard blockade-runners make a haul, but some commanders of Union warships also amassed fortunes in capturing blockade-runners and sharing in the "prize" money. Charles Cowley in *Leaves from a Lawyer's*

Life Afloat and Ashore reported that ladings of the captured runner *Cambria* were valued at $191,000; the blockade-runner *Lodona* became a prize with cargo appraised at $246,000; and the famous *Stettin* was caught after a number of trips with a cargo valued at $226,000.

Financial bonuses rewarded many a Union bluejacket too and helped motivate him on the weary watches. Upon the capture of a blockade-runner, twenty shares of the loot went to the prize vessel responsible. According to numerous reports, the most common percentage in dividing the booty was as follows: captain, 15 percent, other officers 20 percent, petty officers 30 percent, seamen 35 percent.

During the war the United States Treasury Department forked over some $10,000,000 to men of the Union Navy for prize awards. Although the reward money was split many ways, and spent as quickly as it was issued, it helped maintain some degree of order among the Union sailors and gave them some reason for staying alert and on the job.

Besides the large amounts of money received, key officers aboard blockade runners were permitted to speculate on their personally imported cargoes. After having made a profit of 1100 percent on 1000 girdle stays, the famous Hobart-Hampden, alias Captain Hewett, Ridge, Roberts, and other names, agreed on a deal with a trader at Wilmington to import on his next voyage a quantity of *Coffin-screws*, as this particular article was in constant demand and was not manufactured in the South.

Hobart actually purchased a quantity of "Cockle pills" in England for speculative purposes. But as they were unheard of in the Southland he decided to carry them to Nassau, "where everyone was billious from overeating and drinking, on the strength of the fortunes they were making by blockade-running; and there I found an enterprising druggist who gave me two chests of lucifer matches in exchange for my cockles, which matches I ultimately sold in the Confederacy at a very fair profit."

As to other speculation, Hobart usually managed to influence the stevedores, who were loading cotton for the outward-bound voyage, to include a few extra bales "for the captain and officers, those uncontrollable rascals whom the poor agents could not manage."

Certainly Hobart was one blockade-running captain who fared well. He was an able seaman and a daring adventurer. With reference to his blockade-running deeds he commented in his memoirs, "Indeed, putting on one side the sordid motives which I dare say to a certain extent actuated us, there was a thrilling and glorious excitement about the work. . . . One was always either running away or being deliberately pitched into by the broadsides of the American cruisers, the slightest resistance to which would have constituted piracy; whereas capture without resistance merely entailed confiscation of cargo and vessel."

Along with his audacious recklessness, Hobart enjoyed his career. On the occasion of having been caught in an amorous position with the daughter of the governor of a particular British colony, he explained to the indignant official, "Really, general, I hardly know how to answer you. Your daughter and I are very good friends, this place is most detestably dull, there is nothing to do, and if we amuse ourselves with a little love-making, surely there can be no great harm. . . ." He "thought the old boy would have had a fit!"

Following each profitable run Hobart, who was no different from any other blockade-runner, spent money lavishly. There was always an excuse for a party. On one particular occasion after outrunning the Yankees, he recalled:

"Being now perfectly safe, lights were at once lit, supper and grog served out *ad libitum*, everybody congratulated everybody, and a feeling of comfort and jollity, such as can only be experienced after three nights and three days intense anxiety, possessed us all.

"It will be difficult to erase from my memory the excitement of the evening we made our little craft fast alongside the quay at Wilmington; the congratulations we received, the champagne cocktail we imbibed, the eagerness with which we gave and received news. . . . All these things, combined with the delightful feeling of security from capture, and the glorious prospect of a good night's rest in a four-poster, wound one up into an inexpressible state of jollity. If some of us had a little headache in the morning, surely it was small blame to us."

It was a desperate game played by desperate men. However, the game was hardly considered sport by those aboard the runners when Yankee shells began bursting over their heads. Rewards were fantastically high but so were the stakes.

The illustrious Louis Coxetter, captain of the blockade-runner *Herald (Antonica)*, had made so many successful runs that he had been proclaimed by the Federal government "a pirate." Needless to say, he was not particularly anxious to be captured and taken prisoner. And it has been told that on one extremely close call with a Yankee warship gaining on him he seated himself on the ladder leading to the engine room and, with a Colt revolver idly held in his hand, politely informed the chief engineer that he would be a dead man if he couldn't get up more steam.

There is no question that without Union sea power and the blockading of Rebel ports the Confederate States would have succeeded in their goal of obtaining independence. With proper supply lines the image, morale, and fighting strength of the struggling Confederate Army would have been sustained.

But the agricultural economy of the South made supplies from the outside a necessity. And the blockade suppressed this outlet. As Union Naval strength grew, the blockade noose tightened in effectiveness and finally accomplished a stranglehold as important to Union victory as their feats in the field.

In August 1861, Northern vessels with some 800 soldiers launched an amphibious assault on the sand dune Confederate forts at Hatteras Inlet. Although the Unionists were inexperienced, they caught the Rebel defenders unprepared. The batteries at Fort Clark and Fort Hatteras were bombarded with undeserved accuracy. After a short engagement which wounded several dozen on both sides and killed seven Confederates, the white flag went up and the Northern Navy claimed its first major victory. The capture forced the blockade-running trade to choose other inlets and ports. More importantly, it provided the Federals with a much needed supply base on the far reaching Southern shores.

Another Union Naval victory at Port Royal, South Carolina, and the capture of the forts at Hilton Head, in November 1861 gave the North an important harbor vital to the defense of the Southern coast. This loss was one of the first truly serious blows to the Confederacy. Port Royal was one of the well-situated Southern harbors which, because of its many estuaries, was a popular hiding place for blockade-runners. Its central location was most necessary to the Southern cause in the early stages of the war.

Shortly afterward, the occupation of Tybee Island, Georgia, guarding the approach to Savannah, definitely hampered blockade-running activities in and out of that port.

In December 1861, Beaufort, South Carolina, was abandoned to the Federals, and the Northern papers boasted confidently that their amazing sea power had crushed the hopes of the South forever.

By early spring 1862, a number of coastal towns in eastern North Carolina had fallen, as had Norfolk and Hampton Roads. At the end of April 1862, the Union fleet under Flag Officer David Farragut destroyed the Confederate flotilla defending New Orleans, which led to the surrender of the South's wealthiest city. However, Albert Sidney Johnston with 30,000 men had repulsed Grant with 70,000 at Shiloh. Almost 3500 Union and Confederate soldiers died on this battlefield. And June 1862 witnessed the vicious Seven Days' Battles in which Lee drove off Grant, much to the relief of Richmond. However, the series of bloody engagements cost the Confederates 19,739 men killed and wounded.

Although the successes of the Rebel Army set the Southern people delirious with joy, Lee realized his men were growing weaker by the month. Many of his reinforcements had disappeared into the grave, the hospital, or deserted for home.

As more and more seaboard havens of blockade-runners came under the Stars and Stripes, only a few ports were left through which the Confederacy could receive its desperately needed supplies.

General Robert E. Lee hit the nail on the head in an official dispatch, ". . . we have no guns that can resist their batteries . . . the strength of the enemy can be thrown with great celerity against any point, and far outnumbers any force we can bring against it." His words rang true, and on September 6, 1863, Morris Island at the entrance to Charleston Harbor was abandoned by stanch Confederate forces after suffering through two months of fierce bombardment.

Spring 1864 saw the South still bolstering its countenance. Lee with only half an army had battered Grant at the Battle of the Wilderness and Spottsylvania. Grant still was to suffer his bloodiest loss at Cold Harbor in June.

Confederate newspapers reported the battles "in which the Yankees were defeated with great slaughter." They showered enthusiastic praise upon the gallantry of the brilliant Confederate defense. Yet, day by day the Unionists drew closer to Richmond. The dreadful losses had brought Lee's once formidable army to a low state of morale and discipline. His men were reduced to a frazzle.

Although most of the Confederacy held its ground, the Yankees controlled the coastal sections of Louisiana and the Mississippi River, as well as a number of key forts at Hampton Roads, Chesapeake Bay, and along the Atlantic and Gulf Coasts.

By the end of the summer, however, Sherman had taken Atlanta. Farragut had steamed through the deadly torpedo field at Mobile and won a fierce battle overcoming Fort Morgan and Fort Gaines. This left Gulf of Mexico ports all but closed to the blockade-runners. From this time until the end of it all, Wilmington became the principal Confederate port. General Lee's 33,000 starved, ragged heroes in the trenches around Petersburg, and General Johnston's 25,000 weary men in North Carolina, desperately depended upon the blockade-runners that ran to Wilmington. In essence, Wilmington was as important to the Confederacy as Richmond, if not more so.

L. E. Chittenden, in *Recollections of President Lincoln and His Administration*, refers to the state of conditions of most of the Confederate Army as he describes one Rebel soldier he confronted in July 1864: "I had not forgotten the sharp shooter 'winged' by the target rifle. There, behind the log he lay, on his back . . . with a peaceful expression on his rugged face. His rifle and cartridge box were of English make, and were the only things about him which did not indicate extreme destitution. . . .

"His feet, wrapped in rags, had coarse shoes upon them, so worn and full of holes that they were only held together by means of pieces of thick twine. Ragged trousers, a jacket, a shirt of what used to be called 'tow cloth,' a straw hat, which had lost a large portion of both crown and rim, completed his attire. His hair was a mat of dust and grime; his face and body were thickly coated with dust and dirt, which gave him the color of red Virginia clay.

"A haversack hung from his shoulder. Its contents were a jack knife, a plug of twisted tobacco, a tin cup, and about two quarts of coarsely cracked corn with, perhaps, an ounce of salt, tied in a rag. . . . This was a complete inventory of the belongings of one Confederate soldier. . . ."

In December 1864, Thomas E. Taylor, a principal in a blockade running business, was summoned to Richmond by the Commissary General of the Confederate Army, who told Taylor under the promise of secrecy that "Lee's army was in terrible straits, and had in fact rations only for about thirty days."

Asked if he could help, Taylor replied that he would do his utmost, and as he later stated in his book, *Running the Blockade*, "after some negotiations he undertook to pay me a profit of 350 percent upon any provisions and meat I could bring in within the next three weeks."

In his memoirs Taylor said, "I had then, discharging in Wilmington, the *Banshee II*, which had just been sent out to replace the first *Banshee* * and [upon returning to Wilmington] I successfully ran the blockade out, purchased my cargo of provisions etc. at Nassau for about $30,000 for which eventually I was paid over $135,000, and after a most exciting run in, landed the same at Wilmington within eighteen days after leaving Richmond."

In 1864 the blockade-running business was at its peak. Now, the South depended on the speedy little vessels more

* The *Banshee I* made eight round trips in safety. Mr. Taylor then had to go to Richmond on business connected with the contracts his firm had entered into with the Confederate government. On the ninth voyage *Banshee I* was captured after a long chase off Cape Hatteras. But she had earned enough on her eight successful round trips to pay the owners 700 percent on their investment.

than ever. Much to the chagrin of the Union Navy, as well as Lincoln himself, the silhouettes of one runner after another appeared almost nightly as they passed through the Cape Fear River bringing supplies to Wilmington.

Rear Admiral John A. Dahlgren, Commander of the South Atlantic Blockading Squadron, wrote Gideon Welles, U.S. Secretary of the Navy, in June 1864 regarding blockade-running into Charleston Harbor, ". . . a perfect blockade was thus enforced, so that the illicit trade of the city was completely cut off."

However, Charles Cowley, who was Judge Advocate of the same South Atlantic Blockading Squadron, later wrote in his *Leaves from a Lawyer's Life Afloat and Ashore*, "The fact is, blockade-running was not stopped, and never could be wholly stopped without more vessels than Dahlgren ever had until after the fall of Wilmington. There are six different channels to Charleston, of such configuration that vessels of light draught, taking advantage of dark nights, could elude the vigilance of the blockading fleet."

It is true that the Union blockade never could totally stop Confederate blockade-running. But it did cut the flow of vital goods to a mere trickle, as the chances of a successful voyage into the blockaded coast became increasingly slimmer. The North later had a great many additional steamers in action, and at times it appeared that the sea was literally covered with warships. Many blockade-runners were picked up during the daytime in open ocean loaded with heavy cargoes of cotton.

Before the first month of 1865 passed, Fort Fisher fell. The event marked the largest amphibious operation in American history until World War II. Equally significant, this was the last blockade-running stronghold of the South. It was the entrance to Wilmington.

By the middle of February 1865, Charleston was evacuated and blockade-running was at an end. On February 18,

four do-or-die runners headed into Charleston Harbor un-
aware of the fate of that city. The steamers *Celt, Deer, Lady
Davis,* and *Syren* all were captured.

Captain Wilkinson, himself, in *Narrative of a Blockade
Runner,* reminisced about his despair at not being able to
enter Charleston as that city was under bombardment. He
had spent five days at sea from Nassau eluding Union warships. He recalled, "As this was the last night during that
moon, when the bar could be crossed during dark hours,
the course of the *Chameleon* was again, and for the last
time, shaped for Nassau. As we turned away from land, our
hearts sank within us, while the conviction forced itself
upon us, that the cause for which so much blood had been
shed, so many miseries bravely endured, and so many sac-
rifices cheerfully made, was about to perish at last."

The blockade-running captains and merchants who withdrew early from the business acquired considerable sums of
money. But those who continued to the end encountered
heavy losses. When an investment speculation brings sudden profit, it will more than likely be overdone. The happy
investor usually goes overboard and becomes involved in an
excessive way. And so it was with blockade-running. A
large amount of capital was still being invested in blockade-
running companies when most of the South was ready to admit defeat. Even in March 1865, Confederate authorities
were launching one last, hopeless plot. It was planned to
run two steamers loaded with supplies up the James River,
as well as the York River. This would be the last chance of
refurbishing General Lee. But Lee was forced by Grant's
unfaltering persistence to abandon Richmond before the
scheme could be put to work. He retreated to Appomattox.

When blockade-running collapsed, the South collapsed.

Today there are hundreds of wrecked blockade-runners
lying on the bottom of the ocean. Their names, their crews,
their cargoes, and their amazing histories have been forgot-

ten. Even the old-timers who have known since their childhood about an "ol' wreck off th' beach 'bout there," cannot
tell you the name of her, nor do they know the significance
of the sunken hulk.

There are a few, though, who do. They know about the
last days of the *Ella;* the fate of the *Phantom;* the gold
aboard the *Beauregard;* the rifles on the *Ranger;* the legend
of the *Venus:* the horrible crime associated with the loss of
Georgiana McCaw; and the drunken pilot of the blockade-
runner *Vesta.*

The shoreline south from Beaufort, North Carolina, to
Savannah, Georgia, is littered with rusting remains of
wrecked blockade-runners. The greatest number of shipwrecks can be found along the beaches near Cape Fear
where they ran aground while trying to reach the harbor of
Wilmington. The entrance to Charleston Harbor also marks
the final resting place of some of the "gray ghosts."

II

CAPE FEAR'S
FEARLESS FLEET

"It is the playground of billows and tempests, the kingdom of silence and awe, disturbed by no sound save the sea gull's shriek and the breaker's roar. Its whole aspect is suggestive, not of repose and beauty, but of desolation and terror. Imagination cannot adorn it. Romance cannot hallow it. Local pride cannot soften it. There it stands . . . and there it will stand bleak and threatening and pitiless until the earth and the sea shall give up their dead. And as its nature, so its name, is now, always has been, and always will be the Cape of Fear."

CHAPTER 2

Crossroads of the Confederacy

Smith Island marks the entrance to the Cape Fear River. Some twenty miles upstream lies the port of Wilmington, North Carolina. Smith Island has not changed much since the blockade-running days, or even before that century-old era. It still has its sand dunes and pine trees and desolate wastes of swampland heavily populated with green-head flies and fat mosquitoes. Surf fishing generally is good near the point, from which Frying Pan Shoals extend some twenty-five miles seaward.

From a mariner's position the Cape of Fear always has ben a treacherous point to pass beyond. The land lies low and is not easily seen until a ship is close up. Then, it may be too late. The shoals are ever present, and water depths can change noticeably overnight from shifting sands and varying currents.

The Gulf Stream passes near here, and with it have come ships since the beginning of commerce in the New World. Heavily laden vessels of Spanish plate fleets grounded on the shoals, as have trading craft of every nation. German submarines took heavy toll on ships of the Merchant Marine during the World Wars, and even a pirate captain or two used the numerous local inlets as a refuge and campsite.

Stede Bonnet was spotted by the South Carolinian Colonel Rhett while anchored in the lee of Smith Island. The fight that led to the pirate's capture took place in the Cape Fear River in 1718. The rumor was that Bonnet, not wanting to be caught with incriminating evidence, had buried his loot on the island before doing battle. If a Confederate soldier on patrol did not discover the treasure, it may still be there.

Today, Wilmington is a progressive North Carolina city. Its history has long been associated with the sea, but, more than that, the city and its people surround themselves with tradition and historical sentiment. Even in casual contacts the city reflects an old-fashioned courtesy.

However, the conservative old town was turned upside down during the Civil War. Much like Charleston, South Carolina, Wilmington attracted speculators of every type who loved the South because of the capital gain they could realize in support of the "cause." English shipowners and representatives of large mercantile houses took over the town and were notoriously extravagant in the way they entertained "any and everybody."

Blockade-running traffic grew rapidly as agents and traders moved into Wilmington. Warehouses were constructed along the waterfront. Steam cotton presses were put in operation near Beery's shipyard for use in compressing cotton into bales in preparation for shipment abroad. The meager rail connections soon were being constantly overworked in shipping war supplies throughout the Confederate States.

The natural advantages of Wilmington for blockade-running favored this Southern port more so than others. Wilmington, because of its geographic location at the "Crossroads of the South," was better situated for supplying troops in Virginia where most of the fighting was done.

Its rail connections provided reasonable access to other prime sectors of the Confederacy. However, of most importance to the pilots of blockade-runners was the fact that at the approach to Wilmington there were two separate channels leading to the Cape Fear River. A pilot could take his pick according to the position of the Union fleet. He might choose either New Inlet, near Fort Fisher, or the Western Bar route to the South which marked the entrance to the Cape Fear River. Depending upon the circumstances of wind, weather, and the location of the fleet, a crafty runner pilot would select the proper entrance at the precise moment and dash for it with full steam.

These two entrances were only seven miles apart, as the crow flies, but almost forty miles by sea, because of the dreaded Frying Pan Shoals that extend seaward from Cape Fear. This distance factor made the coast difficult to defend from the viewpoint of the Yankee Navy and explains, partly, why the Federals were never able completely to control blockade-running. From Smithville, North Carolina (now Southport), a small village almost equidistant from either entrance, the inner blockading fleet was usually visible. This permitted those runners that were outward bound to make a choice between which passage they would use to run the gauntlet.

It was common practice to station two rows of blockading warships off the entrances to Wilmington. The first line of blockaders was spread close to shore, just beyond reach of the Confederate batteries. The second squadron patrolled an area some twenty to forty miles out. If the outer blockading patrol spotted an unidentified craft they immediately gave chase and sent up rockets or fired their guns as a signal to the inshore vessels on station near the inlets.

Once having bypassed the outside blockade and gained an "inside" advantage, blockade-runners hugged the shore. With a background of shadowy sand dunes they were practically invisible, even on clear nights. Sometimes they would anchor in a neighboring inlet while waiting for the proper tide. At times, contraband cargo was offloaded in the lee of such inlets as Masonboro, Rich, or Topsail. Once under way, the noise of the wind and surf would almost eliminate sounds of a runners' engine or wheels.

James Sprunt, noted Southern historian who lived in Wilmington, recalled back in 1896 some of the qualifications and skills of those who ran the blockade: "The Cape Fear pilots have long maintained a standard of excellence in their profession most creditable to them as a class, and as individuals. The story of their wonderful skill and bravery in the time of the Federal blockade has never been written, for the survivors are modest men, and time has obliterated from their memories many incidents of this extraordinary epoch. Amidst impenetrable darkness, without lightship or beacon, the narrow and closely watched inlet was felt for with a deep-sea lead as a blind man feels his way along a familiar path, and even when the enemy's fire was raking the wheelhouse, the faithful pilot, with steady hand, and iron nerve, safely steered the little fugitive of the sea to her desired haven. It might be said of him, as of the Nantucket skipper, that he could get his bearings on the darkest night by the taste of the lead."

Many of the Cape Fear pilots resided in Smithville, now Southport, near the mouth of the Cape Fear River. Even today Southport is home base for the Carolina shrimpers and commercial fishermen. Some of the boat captains, together with others engaged in seafaring activities of that region, recall stories of their forefathers who played key roles in running the Federal blockade. (Many of them, however, are tight-lipped about disclosing family secrets regarding their blockade-running ancestors.)

In his *Chronicles of the Cape Fear River*, Sprunt refers to an old friend and veteran pilot of blockade-running days, James William Craig, who later became a Methodist Minister: ". . . But I like to think of him as Jim Billy, the Cape Fear pilot of war times, on the bridge of the swift Confed-

erate blockade-runner *Lynx* commanded by the intrepid
Captain Reed, as she races through the blackness of night on
her course west nor'west, straight and true for the Federal
fleet off New Inlet, in utter silence, the salt spray of the sea
smiting the faces of the watch as they gaze ahead for the
first sign of imminent danger.

"Soon there is added to the incessant noise of wind and
waves the ominous roar of the breakers as the surf complains
to the shore, and the deep-sea lead gives warning of shoaling
water. 'Half speed,' is muttered through the speaking tube;
a hurried parley; a recognized landfall—for Reed is a fine
navigator—and 'Are you ready to take her, Pilot?' 'Ready,
sir,' comes from Jim Billy in the darkness. Then he whispers
orders through the tube: 'Slow down'; as there looms ahead
the first of the dread monsters of destruction. 'Starboard,'
'Steady,' and the little ship glides past like a phantom, unseen as yet. Then 'Port,' 'Port,' 'Hard a-port' in quick suc-
cession, as she almost touches the second cruiser. She is
now in the thick of the blockading squadron; and suddenly,
out of the darkness and close aboard, comes the hoarse hail,
'Heave to, or I'll sink you,' followed by a blinding glare of
rockets and the roar of heavy guns. The devoted little Confederate is now naked to her enemies, as the glare of rockets
and Drummond lights from many men-of-war illuminate
the chase. Under a pitiless hail of shot and shell from every
quarter, she bounds full speed ahead, every joint and rivet
straining, while Jim Billy dodges her in and out through a
maze of smoke and flame and bursting shells. The range of
Fort Fisher's guns is yet a mile away. Will she make it? Onward speeds the little ship, for neither Reed nor Jim Billy
has a thought of surrender. A shell explodes above them,
smashing the wheelhouse; another shell tears away the starboard paddle-box; and as she flies like lightning past the
nearest cruiser, a sudden roar from Colonel Lamb's artillery
warns her pursuers that they have reached their limitations;

and in a few minutes the gallant little ship crosses the bar and anchors under the Confederate guns. The Captain and his trusty pilot shake hands and go below, 'to take the oath,' as Reed described it—for the strain must be relaxed by sleep or stimulation. 'A close shave, Jim,' was all the Captain said. 'It was, sir, for a fact,' was the equally laconic answer."

CHAPTER 3

A Little Bloke in a Stovepipe Hat

The trip to Bermuda was, I thought, just another one of those disasters.

For five days I had waited for the weather to clear. I had come to the island to shoot underwater footage on a Spanish galleon whose bones had just been found on the outer reefs, but the wind and heavy seas began on the day I arrived. Now, on the fifth day of my frustration, I was loafing in a small pub near the harbor at St. George's. As the afternoon droned along, I assumed a light cargo of pale ale and stout to keep the day from being a total loss.

The bar's clientele was a mixed bag of tourists and seafaring men, good-natured and bantering, and somehow I was drawn into a small group of English sailors who rolled dice for a round of drinks. That was how I met George Winston.

He was short and chunky, somewhere between forty-five and sixty, with skin that had once been fair but now was blotched like tattered leather by a generation at sea. Thinning sandy hair grew loosely in brief curls above where his neck should have been. When he talked, the words rolled out in puffs, almost explosively, in a high-pitched rendition of classic Limehouse.

He was a willing conversationalist, spurred on, perhaps, by several pints of St. Pauli Girl beer. When he learned I was a diver it was impossible to quiet him. As a former Royal Navy stoker he claimed to know the graves of many ships, still bearing valuable cargo, that German torpedoes had sent to the bottom. I had heard of most of them.

We talked for an hour or so, and then Winston said he must return to his ship, a creaky British freighter he served as boatswain. He drained the last of his mug and turned to me with an afterthought as he made ready to leave. Little did I dream that his chance remark would start me on a new road of adventure and be, in fact, the basis for this book.

"Tell you what, mate," he said, "if you'd like to meet a *real* expert on shipwrecks, I'll take you to one. He's our first mate [Winston pronounced it 'fahrst mite'] and you've no idea the information the man carries in his head."

Winston said the mate was still aboard their freighter. I protested, feebly, "He probably wouldn't want to be bothered."

My raffish Cockney friend persisted, "Listen, man," said he, positively, "Mr. Gamble has passed more buoys than you have telephone poles. Come along!" Well, I thought, at least I might collect a few good yarns to carry home. I certainly wasn't going back with any film.

"Okay," I agreed, "lead the way."

We picked our way through the usual dockside tangle until we came to Winston's freighter. Probably it had looked good in the twenties. Now it was gnawed cruelly by the years, and I recalled with irony Masefield's line about "great steamers white and gold." It was hard to imagine that this one was ever anything but old.

The first mate was well suited to his ship.

We found him in the chart room, with a mug of black coffee before him; motionless, his hooded eyes seemed turned back in time and space. To where? I wondered. Apparently he was well past normal retirement age. There was such an air of ruin about him that I was startled at the vigor of his speech when he rose and responded to Winston's introduction. Obviously, he was not as decrepit as he looked.

Mr. Gamble (I never knew his first name) was as tall and courtly as Winston was short and coarse. At first he seemed embarrassed that the boatswain had brought me aboard to meet him as if, perhaps, he had been a curiosity at an exhibition. Yet he warmed to the occasion and we talked at some length of shipwrecks around the world.

At one point I mentioned that I was from Virginia.

"Well then," he said, "you're close to North Carolina. I have heard remarkable stories of many an iron steamer which grounded near Cape Fear while running the blockade during the American Civil War. I understand that some of these hulks are still visible. Is that correct?"

"To some extent, yes," I replied. "The *Beauregard* could be seen not long ago in the breakers off Carolina Beach, and the *Ranger* often is visible at low tide near Lockwood's Folly inlet. And there are others, too. Occasionally, strong tides reveal unknown wreck remains."

The old sailor paused a moment, as if he were weighing my comments on a scale of memories. Reaching thoughtfully for his mug of coffee he asked, "And those wrecks which have been uncovered by recent storms . . . have you investigated them?"

"Not with any real effort, sir," I answered. "Most sunken ships in our region are in such a state of disintegration that they are practically unidentifiable. Always assumed there was nothing of any value on them anyway," I added. "Especially on those sunk so close to shore."

He pressed the coffee mug to his lips and took a long gulp. With his eyes fixed upon me his stare gradually changed to an easy, wrinkled grin. "Nothing aboard them, eh!" he mused. "Then you've never dived on one?"

I shook my head. "No, but I know two brothers from Wilmington, North Carolina, who have. All they've found so far was a few pigs of lead."

"Aye, lead, by all means," he said. "There'd be plenty of that. But gold too, my boy. At least on one of them.

"I have no authentic knowledge, of course. But as a lad I knew an old sailor in Liverpool who had run the blockade many times in 1863 and '64. His name was Harry Montgomery. When I knew him he was almost blind. He lived in a row house not far off Lime Street, and in good weather he would sit out on the steps and spin sea stories by the hour. Much as I'm doing now." The old mate cast a salty look at Winston and me, and laughed.

"Aye, we all love a good yarn, Mr. Gamble," Winston chirped. "It's part of the game."

"Well," Gamble said, "lots of them are so much hot air. We all know that. And for years I thought old Montgomery was full of it, too. But now and then I would stumble on some genuine facts, about some ship or other, or some event, and it would all sound familiar. And I would recall hearing substantially the same tale from old man Montgomery.

"For example, he talked often about serving under a Captain Burgoyne who ran the blockade into Wilmington. To hide his true identity, Burgoyne assumed an alias as Captain Talbot in command of the blockade-runner *Elsie*. Burgoyne was a British naval officer on leave to the merchant service.* After the war, he commanded an experimental ironclad— the *Captain*—which sank in a storm in the Bay of Biscay in

---

* The *Elsie* was a swift, new steamer whose career was cut short by a shell from the U.S.S. *Quaker City* on duty in the Gulf of Mexico. According to *Official Records*, no less than 120 shots had been fired at *Elsie* before she surrendered.

1870. Burgoyne was drowned, with many of his crew. Well, as I later learned, that's exactly what happened. Doesn't really mean anything, of course, except as an example that much of what old Montgomery told I was later able to verify.

"Now as to the gold. Montgomery claimed to have run the blockade in several ships, but he was particularly fond of one called *Phantom*. Nearly as I can recall he described her as a screw steamer of about five hundred tons. She would cruise at sixteen knots and could do eighteen if pressed. Not bad for 1863. This rust bucket we're aboard now makes only fifteen. Like all the blockade-runners, *Phantom* was long and low, and was painted a gray-white shade.

"As Montgomery told it, *Phantom*—with a Captain Porter commanding—was running for Wilmington from Bermuda. Somewhere off the North Carolina coast she was spied by a United States gunboat and pursued. It was still a long way to Wilmington and the cruiser was fast.

"Now it seems there was a passenger aboard, a little bloke in a stovepipe hat, who had stayed close to his cabin for most of the four-day trip. Montgomery thought he was a Confederate agent returning to Dixie on some special mission. Anyhow, when things were looking desperate for the *Phantom*, he grew much alarmed and buzzed about the captain, gesturing frantically.

"Captain Porter decided the game was up. *Phantom* was cut off and being forced closer to land. It was either surrender to the cruiser or run aground, as close to the beach as possible, so there would be some chance of shore parties salvaging the cargo. If that looked doubtful they could set her afire."

Mr. Gamble fished for a Players cigarette, and stirred sugar into a fresh mug of coffee. I could sense him groping back through the years. I tried to picture a street in Liverpool where an old sailor spun yarns for small boys who clustered around his steps.

"Having passed the decisive word to his crew the skipper made straight for his cabin," the old mate continued. "The strange passenger disappeared below deck. Swiftly Master Porter gathered some papers from his desk and placed them in a leather dispatch case crammed with other documents. Yankee shells began exploding all around.

"Calling Montgomery to his side, Captain Porter gave instructions to secure a line around his dispatch case and lower it to the water's edge. About that time the Confederate agent returned topside, staggering under the weight of a small, but obviously heavy, strongbox. The Captain ordered Montgomery to make the line fast to the box and both units were lowered away. If the gunboat caught up with them before they beached, Montgomery was to cut the line and send the valuables to Davy Jones.

"Old Harry Montgomery always enjoyed telling this part of his story. In fact, he'd go into great detail about the way he stood on that starboard quarter, shot and shell whistling past his ears, with his right hand wielding a fire ax and his left grasping that most important line which strained in a rusty cleat against a hastily made half hitch. He claimed to have aged ten years in ten minutes, during those hot moments.

"But *Phantom* grounded before she was caught. She hit the shoals head on at eighteen knots. It must have been one hell of a jolt. Before she was well settled the crew had fires burning fore and aft. Then they stuffed their pockets with bottles of rum and brandy and made for the boats.

"The commander ordered all boats off save the one close to Montgomery, still standing by with his ax. Then they lowered, with six seamen and the Confederate passenger inside. Porter, Montgomery, and another sailor were the last to abandon *Phantom*.

"The idea was to get the boat directly under the dangling items and then swing them aboard. Montgomery had let loose the heavy line and was paying it over the gunwale. Then two things happened at once. A breaker struck the ship—shoving the lifeboat off its position—and a direct hit from the Yankee cruiser struck one of *Phantom*'s stacks. It exploded and fragments of steel showered everywhere.

"The three men were knocked to the deck. Montgomery said his head cleared just in time to see the end of the line snaking over the side. Strongbox and dispatch case went to the bottom like so many stones.

"Well, Captain Porter and Montgomery made it safely into the boat and to shore. As he told the story, Montgomery said the Captain just clenched his jaw and didn't say a word all the way to the beach.

"The Confederate chap, he said, sat in the boat wringing his hands and shaking his head. He would look back at *Phantom* and say, over and over, 'Lord help me now.' But here's the good part. When they were safely on dry land he turned to Montgomery and said in a voice quivering with emotion: 'Well, my man, you've just let forty-five thousand in gold slip through your bungling fingers.'

"I can still hear old Montgomery laughing," Mr. Gamble said. "He liked that yarn. I rather do myself."

Winston and I did, too. I wanted to know more, of course: Was there any indication the gold had been recovered? What else was in the captain's dispatch case? Why was the gold being brought into the Confederacy (usually it was going the other way)? Above all, did Mr. Gamble really think the story was true?

The old sailor chuckled softly. It had grown quite dark, and the shadows etched deep creases in his thin face. His eyes gleamed from dark hollows.

"I just don't know, mate," he said. "That's all I remember. But if you're a diver, as you say you are, why don't you find out for yourself?"

Winston showed me to the gangway. We had become good friends in a short while, and I sensed he appreciated my companionship.

"Do you really think the old fellow knows what he's talking about?" I asked. "His story is fantastic."

Winston grinned and extended a stubby hand.

"You have to give the man credit," he said, "I've never known anyone to prove him wrong."

Walking back to my hotel that night I stopped to look out across the silent harbor. Perhaps it was on just such a night that *Phantom* had cleared this very port for Wilmington.

I wondered if there really had been a mysterious passenger in a stovepipe hat, who stayed close to his cabin, guarding a heavy box. I wondered, but there was one thing I knew.

Someday I would try to find the *Phantom*.

The telephone rang on a Thursday evening in May of 1964.

"The weather looks good, pal," said the voice on the other end. "You can start getting your gear together. That is, if you're still interested in diving on the *Phantom*."

The voice belonged to Hall Watters of Wilmington. I had known Hall and his brother, Robert, for several years, and in the year that had elapsed since my Bermuda trip I had urged them to see if *Phantom*'s wreck could be located. A short time before the telephone call he had written that the hulk had been found and positively identified.

Hall rattled on about the weather as my excitement mounted.

"We've got a high pressure area here and a light southerly breeze. She'll be swinging around to the southeast by tomorrow. That means clear water at New Topsail by Saturday."

"Great," I said. "Make motel reservations for me at the usual place. And hang onto that high pressure area for a few days." By this time my wife, Jayne, who had been near the kitchen telephone, had caught the drift of my conversation. She threw up her hands in a melodramatic show of disgust.

"I'll do it, mate," Hall said. "And let's get an early start. I'll pick you up at the motel at four A.M."

The 250-mile trip from Richmond to Wilmington that Friday afternoon seemed even longer than usual. The hot, flat, clay-smeared face of that part of eastern North Carolina was hardly scenic, and I occupied my mind with thoughts of all I had been able to learn about the story of *Phantom*'s last cruise.

Obviously, the old mate's tale in Bermuda had made a deep impression on me, and I couldn't forget the blockade runner and her mystery gold. Throughout the winter I had researched Civil War books and records. Some were recent; others were new reprints of classic editions or volumes dating from the late 1860s and the 1870s, musty with age. I was even fortunate enough to locate some original records of the wartime period. All the while, the thin face and hollowed eyes of Mate Gamble haunted my memory and spurred me on.

Each piece of information gradually began to fit together. The gigantic puzzle was almost complete. Amazingly, each authentic detail I found seemed to tie in perfectly, one way or another, with the story of the old sailor.

The *Phantom* was a real ship; there was no mistake about that. She was a sleekly handsome iron-plated vessel of 170 horsepower and was one of the few blockade-runners owned by the Confederacy. *Phantom* was a perfect name for her when she came out of a Liverpool shipyard in late

1862, painted a dull gray-white and her hull showing only five feet above the water. She was rated at 500 tons; her length was 190 feet and her beam only 22. Her draft was a mere eight feet six inches. She carried a crew of 33 and, just as Mr. Gamble had said, she could steam at a then-miraculous 18 knots.

With her low silhouette, camouflaging paint job, and the smokeless anthracite coal that she burned, *Phantom* was practically invisible at 200 yards. Her boats were carried square with the gunwales to further decrease visibility. A steamer of utter silence, she even "blew her tubes" underwater to keep from making any telltale noise.

Phantom left Liverpool in early April of 1863 under the command of S. G. Porter, an experienced skipper regarded as a man of "coolness, courage, and good seamanship."

The new ship ran the blockade successfully three times. And on one trip from Wilmington to Bermuda she carried the most glamorous Confederate agent of all.

Rose O'Neal Greenhow was sailing for England with the private and official blessing of Jefferson Davis. This vital, dark-haired widow already had rendered great help to the Confederacy: now she was to act as an unofficial ambassador to England (and to some extent France) and try to bolster the South's sagging prestige in the wake of Gettysburg. She had written a book about the Confederacy, too. In England, she could have it published and it would help the cause.

Mrs. Greenhow sailed on *Phantom* on August 5, 1863, after writing Davis of her surprise at the number of blockade-running types hanging about Wilmington "who ought to be in the army." She also told the President:

"The Yankees are reported as being unusually vigilant, a double line of blockaders block the way. Still, I am nothing daunted and hope by the blessing of Providence to get out in safety."

That prayer, at least, was answered, although the luck of Rebel Rose would end aboard another blockade-runner, *Condor* by name. For now, she was safe, with still more service to the Confederacy (and personal romance) ahead. At Bermuda she transferred to a British man-of-war for the voyage to England, certainly V.I.P. treatment, probably at the instigation of President Davis himself.

Mrs. Greenhow safely delivered, *Phantom* made another trip to the Confederacy; then returned to Bermuda on September 15, 1863, to offload cotton and take on another valuable cargo for Dixie. Captain Porter gave his crew several days' liberty and sailed September 19 for Wilmington. He was so anxious to depart with the appropriate tide and moon that he refused to delay his schedule for his full load of gunpowder and left with only half of it.

His cargo consisted of "nine cases whiskey, two cases gin, one case wine, 200 pigs lead, two Blakely guns, 50 cases leather, 50 cases Austrian rifles, 135 barrels pork, 150 barrels gunpowder, one case merchandise." *

At daybreak on the morning of September 23 Captain Porter was taking a star sight when a vessel was raised about eight miles distant. He was aware, of course, of his nearness to the North Carolina coast, and his plan was to dash for one of the inlets north of Fort Fisher (the huge earthwork guarding one of the two entrances to the Cape Fear River) and await darkness. Then he would sneak along the coast and slip into New Inlet; thence to the Cape Fear River and Wilmington, twenty miles upstream.

The wind was blowing freshly from the northeast, and it required longer than usual to get a true sight on the yawing deck of the slender runner. He found, though, that *Phantom*'s location was some twelve miles offshore of New River Inlet and about sixty miles northeast of Fort Fisher.

---

* From the original cargo manifest located in the National Archives, Washington, D.C.

Suddenly the vessel viewed in the distance began taking on the alarming characteristics of a Yankee cruiser.

Phantom put on all available steam and changed course to the northwestward. After running in that direction for about two hours, it was obvious that the cruiser was heading them off. Captain Porter made a daring decision to alter his course again. Wheeling around in a 180-degree turn, *Phantom* streaked southward, running all the while close along the coast. At one point breakers were encountered off their port quarter. By 8:00 A.M. shells were splashing around them. The situation was extremely critical, and it grew rapidly worse. Captain Porter decided to beach *Phantom* in the hope that her cargo could be boated ashore.

Phantom grounded just as hard as she ran. The crew set her afire fore and aft and headed for shore. The Union gunboat was now only a mile away and making fast preparation to lower its own boats, all the while firing furious rounds of shot and shell at the escaping Rebels.

By the time the Union crew reached her, all of *Phantom*'s men were on the beach. The vessel burned fiercely, preventing the boarding party from accomplishing any salvage. The gunboat had been recognized by those ashore as the U.S.S. *Connecticut*. That afternoon, *Connecticut* sent another cutter to destroy the runner's boats lying on the beach. This was a foolish attempt that resulted in death for one sailor, Thomas Donahue, who was cut down by a line of fire from the dunes beyond the beach. At this juncture the crew of the cutter did not hesitate to retreat to the *Connecticut*, which fired a number of rounds into *Phantom* before they left her, a total wreck.

Although a heavy surf was running, the next day Porter led his determined crew back to the smoldering shipwreck. They managed to save some of the machinery and cargo lying about the deck; navigational gear, charts, the ship's compass, and assorted merchandise could be reached. A large portion of her food and whiskey was saved together with sixteen cases of rifles.

Since *Phantom*'s hold was filled with water, very little salvage was made on her primary cargo, and 1200 Austrian muskets still remain aboard today.

By September 29 most of *Phantom*'s crew were ordered to new stations, Commander S. G. Porter left for Richmond to make an official report to Colonel Josiah Gorgas, head of the Ordnance Bureau, Confederate States of America, to which the blockade runner was assigned.

Within a few weeks the wreck of the *Phantom* was forgotten and thus she remained, until now.

I had reached Wilmington, where a balmy May night covered the historic city and offered good weather prospects for tomorrow. As I checked into my motel and turned in, I again reviewed the old mate's tale and compared it with the known facts of *Phantom*'s end. Certainly they didn't conflict.

Suddenly it was 4:00 A.M. and Hall Watters was pounding on my door. I dressed quickly and stumbled out into the darkness to drive my station wagon, with its load of diving gear, out to the hangar where the Watters brothers center their flying and diving operations. As I followed Hall's pickup truck through the deserted streets of Wilmington I gradually awoke to the excitement of the day.

The hangar itself is a relic, and I suppose that might account for some of the sense of discovery that one feels on seeing it for the first time. It was built almost fifty years ago and that was before the world had heard of Rickenbacker and von Richthofen, so from the standpoint of aviation history and its curious way of compressing the years as it spans them, the hangar has been there almost forever.

It stands by itself in total isolation out on the far fringe of Wilmington airport. At least a mile from the cluster of aero-related buildings at the vertex of the runways, it drowses in a field of broom sedge and scrub pines at the end of a rutted trail.

Yet all this is utterly deceptive. The hangar is anything but a nostalgic ruin: it is, in fact, jammed with modern (and well-used) equipment to assist man's passage above, on, and under the sea. There are three fish-spotting Piper Cubs in perfect trim and two other Cubs that seem to be slowly decomposing. Inside the three good Pipers, much of the cockpit space is taken up by electronic gear. A pair of decal eyeballs leer lecherously downward from the side window of one of the planes. There are six boats in the hangar, too, an assortment ranging from a venerable skiff to a cabin cruiser.

The miscellany, apart from these major items, is almost indescribable. Enough tools, probably, to service the entire Mexican Air Force are strewn in all directions—life rafts, tanks, tires, parts of aircraft and boats, battered World War II military cases of who-knows-what. A shortwave radio crackled in the corner of a lounge-office area, almost hidden by pieces of an ancient ship's boiler plucked from the bottom of the sea by my experienced diving companion. A number of odd smells contested for dominance of the hangar air, and one seemed to be winning. The heavy, musty, greasy smell grew stronger as I neared two open vats made from the halves of a fifty-gallon oil drum. Linseed oil! Inside the vats, half-hidden in the stinking oil, lay what appeared to be bundles of dirty sticks encrusted with dark scale. They were gunstocks, dozens of gunstocks—British Enfields and Austrian rifles of the 1860s. Hall had a year earlier recovered them from the wrecks of the blockade-runners *Ranger* and *Modern Greece*.

Jumbled on a large table lay a collection of smaller relics, all bearing the mark of a century on the bottom. These

were retrieved from the resting place of the blockade-runner *Ella*. There were stag-handled carving knives and meat
forks, stacks of spoons, galley ladles, great chunks of white
shirt buttons fused together by the cement of hardened
ashes, brass padlocks (in perfect condition), and a surpris-
ingly modern ship's cabin door-lock with a neat oval knob
still attached. Another clump of buttons was cemented to
the lock—a strange incongruity. Still stranger were hand-
sized lumps whose blackness and rough shape made me
think of coal. But closer inspection revealed the lumps to
be solid masses of ordinary brass pins, thousands of them,
stuck together by the same hardened black paste of ashes
that held the buttons.

I picked some of the pins loose: they fell apart rather
easily, and I scratched one clean with the blade of my jack-
knife. The brass glinted like new.

What Confederate tailor had sighed in frustration when
the pins he expected never arrived?

As we rolled out his Piper Cub, Hall casually tossed the
parachutes into the hangar to make room for me to climb
into the small cockpit. I sat behind the pilot's seat, straddling
the gas tanks.

At the crack of dawn we were under way. After climb-
ing to an altitude of about 500 feet, Hall turned to me and
said, "Hold on." He spun the plane around in the direction
of the airport, explaining that he had not been able to clear
the ice that had formed in the carburetor and he wanted to
be headed in the right direction in case we suddenly lost
our power. I was ready to tell him that it would be perfectly
all right with me if he wanted to go ahead and land, when
we turned again and in minutes were in sight of the coastline.

A maze of shallow waterways wound their way in and
out of the sand flats toward New Topsail Inlet. The sea appeared green and was relatively calm at 5:00 A.M., but sev-

eral isolated whitecaps showed themselves occasionally, and we both knew that a stronger wind would be blowing later in the morning. At an altitude of 900 feet we made several passes near the mouth of the inlet. As we were making our third turn an obvious shadow appeared in the water below us. Clearly outlined was the hull of a vessel about 200 feet long. The wreck lay about 250 yards offshore. Water visibility appeared to be close to fifteen feet, and my heart pounded as we nose-dived on her. We could see the boiler quite plainly and something that looked like a rather large propeller.

As I held onto my stomach, Hall threw out a marker buoy and leveled off the Piper about five feet above the surface of the ocean. He turned and gave me a jaunty grin of success.

As we returned and taxied to the hangar we were met by Hall's brother, Robert, and another fish-spotter pilot. The pair had been busily engaged attaching two Boston whalers to the trailer hitch on their trucks. We loaded the pickups with sixteen 72-cubic-foot bottles of compressed air and other necessary diving gear, including nylon line, steel shackles, stainless steel cable, and lifting bags of various sizes.

We stopped for a quick breakfast before renewing our expedition to the coast. By the time we had launched both boats it was eight o'clock. As we emerged from the inlet we noticed that the wind had increased to about fifteen knots, which certainly was not good news that early in the morning. However, we found the buoy very quickly, and Hall crowed about the accuracy of his dive-bombing. The buoy had hit the water only about eighty feet north of the wreck. Hall maneuvered his whaler directly over the wreck, and we made our down line fast around the shaft of the hundred-year-old hulk. *Phantom* seemed fairly well intact. Water visibility had decreased to about four feet, yet the ancient runner was still one of the most provocative wrecks I had ever seen.

I dropped rapidly to the bottom in about thirty-two feet of water. The ship's boiler stood up about ten feet from the floor of the ocean. Her shaft was clearly visible, and I followed it aft until I came to the large iron screw, fully intact and heavily encrusted with coral and finger sponge. At that point Hall joined me. We followed the contour of the hull, cloaked with marine life, and found her broken just about amidships.

Visibility was now only three feet, and the wind apparently had increased as there was a terrific degree of surge around the upper section of the wreck. Since I had brought my Rolleimarin I positioned myself long enough to take several pictures of Hall hanging to the boiler, all the time knowing they would not turn out well in the murky water. I then returned to the boat to leave the camera and pick up our digging tools, a crowbar and geologic pick. Both boats were being tossed about like chips, and we were aware of the hazards of remaining submerged much longer. However, we had waited too long for this moment and were not going to let the storm gods chase us away so easily.

Returning to the bottom, it took fifteen minutes to find my partner. He had entered the hold near the jagged break in her hull. It was much darker there, and that's why I had missed him. As soon as my eyes became accustomed to the shadows, I saw Hall lying on the bottom throwing sand in every direction. Several eight-pound sheepshead hovered near his uppermost shoulder, hoping he would uncover a morsel of food. I moved in and offered the crowbar. He beckoned excitedly to the hole he had dug. Scattered on the bottom were one, two, four, eight, or even more ingots. They were slightly encrusted and were so heavy I knew they were lead. Moving off about twelve feet I dug an exploratory hole and uncovered more lead, all very neatly stacked as if it had been stored there yesterday.

Chipping away some of the calcified crust revealed the name *Pontifex & Wood London*. Someone tapped on my shoulder, and I turned to find Robert with a length of one-inch nylon line. He took over as I returned to the boat for another tank of air. Hall already had run out and was preparing to reenter as I came to the surface.

The wind was blowing at least eighteen knots now, and we hastily agreed to bring up two pigs of lead and then head for shore. Within twenty minutes we had tugged up our prizes. Each one later weighed in at about 125 pounds, yet when we pulled them into the whaler we were sure they would scale at least 200.

Hall made one last descent to free the down line. I busied myself with the usual chores necessary to keep afloat a small fifteen-footer loaded with sixteen tanks of air and two heavy lead ingots. Suddenly it dawned on me that my partner had not returned to the surface.

Fumbling clumsily with my eighteen-pound weight belt, which already had been removed, I struggled to keep my balance and don my scuba gear. I could feel my pulse pounding in my forehead against the face mask, and my knees began to weaken as I made ready to go after my buddy. The surge had been severe on the bottom, and Hall could have been swept into rough wreckage.

As I plunged overboard Hall broke the surface. Relieved, I helped him into the boat and laughed off his incoherent mumbling about an octopus. But when we both were aboard I found that he was dramatically serious.

"A damn octopus," he said. "There's an octopus in her boiler."

I looked at him unbelievingly. "Have you lost your mind?" I asked. "I've never seen an octopus in these waters."

"Next time you're down, 'podner,'" said he, catching his

breath, "you be sure to take a look in ol' *Phantom*'s boiler. It's not a very big one," he added, "tentacles span only 'bout two feet. But she's for real. I grabbed one tentacle but it was slippery, and the thing took off before I could get a good hold."

Our little boats had taken on so much water that we ran the entire distance back to New Topsail Inlet with drain plugs open. By that time the wind was coming from the northeast quadrant, and everyone had to accept the fact that diving was over for that particular weekend.

So engrossed was I with the discovery of the logstacks of lead ingots that I had completely forgotten to search for other relics, particularly the "small metal box" of Mr. Gamble's story. However, I had plucked a piece of conglomerate from the sand during my search for Hall and had placed it inside my weight belt. It had been overlooked until we reached shore and were cleaning our equipment.

I scraped away the covering of shells and hardened sand, and soon the nature of my find was unmistakable. It was hardly an archaeological milestone. Yet it was precisely the kind of prosaic artifact that is most typical of what a treasure-hunter usually finds.

I had braved the surging currents to bring up a brass curtain rod!

Yet even this homely relic stirred my imagination. Perhaps Mrs. Greenhow had peered under it as she left the Confederacy for the last time. Perhaps it had hung in the captain's cabin and had witnessed Porter's desperate last hours aboard his proud steamer.

Better still, perhaps it had helped shield the furtive actions of a stranger in a stovepipe hat before he disappeared into the mists of an old sailor's tale.

It was something to think about while I waited for the day I could return to *Phantom*.

CHAPTER 4

Careless *Condor* and Rebel Rose

The United States Consul at Halifax, Nova Scotia, was a conscientious soul named M. M. Jackson who funneled a stream of priceles information to Secretary of the Navy Gideon Welles. Consider, for example, his telegram of September 6, 1864:

"British blockade-runner, iron steamer *Condor*, 300 tons, 40 men, arrived here today from Ireland via Bermuda, with very large and valuable cargo. Will take on coal and doubtless proceed to Wilmington. . . ."

Thus the Federal authorities were introduced to a new class of blockade runners capable of showing their heels to almost anything afloat. She was the first of seven new iron ships contracted by the Confederate Navy to British shipyards. *Condor* herself probably was built at Glasgow, Scotland, and certainly she was on her maiden voyage when she arrived at Halifax. We even know the name of her insurance agent: Donald McGregor, of London.

Condor was the ultimate, the nonpareil among blockade-runners. All that had been learned over the past three and one-half years was fashioned into her low-slung hull. Her three short-slanted stacks, her great length (270 feet), contrasted rakishly with her shallow freeboard and narrow beam (24 feet). Forward she wore a turtleback. On her decks were a midship house, two raked and stubby masts, and a poopdeck. Her stern was squared off and her color was light lead, or off-white; in short, she looked much like a small World War II destroyer.

As a ship alone she was interesting enough. But it was two of the personalities aboard who gave *Condor*'s only cruise the flavor of a historical novel.

Mrs. Rose Greenhow had completed one year abroad since steaming out of Wilmington aboard *Phantom*. Typically, it was a full year, replete with glittering occasions at the seats of the mighty, great opportunities for her to promote the Confederate cause. Her book, *My Imprisonment and the First Year of Abolition Rule in Washington*, was published in England and sold well. She became intimate with leading political and literary figures and, in the words of Lady Fullerton:

> She poured in English statesmen's ears
> Her pleadings for the South. . . .
>
> Fierce was her glance, and fierce her words,
> She loathed the northern foe;
> With that intensity of hate,
> Impassioned women know.

Yet there were softening influences. The cultured atmosphere of English society; a stay in Paris (where she became a favorite of the French court); most of all, a romance with the recently widowed Lord Granville, culminating in their engagement, brought the flush of beauty back to the still-seductive, fortyish widow. The decision to leave her brilliant circle of new friends must have been a difficult one, and it was a measure of the spirit of this indomitable woman. But pitiful letters from the South told of clothing and food shortages among her friends there: she determined to return to Dixie with as many supplies for them as she could bring through the blockade. Moreover, she had important information to convey to President Davis regarding the Confederacy's business and political status abroad.

It would be a quick trip. She would return to England, and marry Granville.

On August 10, 1864, *Condor* sailed from Greenock, Scotland, with Rebel Rose aboard and keeping a sharp eye on her personal cargo of clothing for women of the South. Observant fellow passengers may have noted that she wore a leather purse, called a reticule, suspended from her neck by a chain, and may have wondered at its contents.

Running the blockade always meant risk, and therefore apprehension. But we may assume that *Condor*'s passengers felt less leery than the average voyagers inbound to Dixie. After all, wasn't their ship the best thing afloat, able to outrun the whole Yankee fleet? Didn't she have a sharp, veteran crew? And the captain—well, wasn't he that prince of blockade-runners, the redoubtable chameleon himself, Augustus Charles Hobart-Hampden?

In the Baltic in 1854 when facing the Russian fleet in command of Her Majesty's Ship *Driver* he had become renowned for his order, "Lads, sharpen your cutlasses!" And once in Buenos Aires he found himself in an equally challenging predicament: "My love affair proved of a more serious nature, at least in its results . . . because, while the daughter responded to my affection, her mother, a handsome woman of forty, chose to fall in love with me herself."

Consider the letter to Secretary Seward from another United States Consul, Thomas Kirkpatrick, at Nassau, dated September 24, 1864. The last paragraph read:

"I understand that officers of the British Navy are now running as blockade runners, and have been. A Captain Roberts, formerly captain of a blockade steamer *Don*, was absent as a post captain in the British Navy on a furlough, that when the furlough expired he went to England and had it extended and is now in Bermuda, or about there. His name in the Navy Register is supposed to be Hobert or Herbert."

He was a tall, bearded sea dog who delighted in confounding the opposition by adopting almost as many aliases as he made voyages through the Yankee blockade. In truth, Augustus Charles Hobart-Hampden was a son of the sixth Earl of Buckinghamshire, a Victoria Cross recipient (from heroic action in the Crimean War) who once was skipper of Queen Victoria's yacht. On various occasions he is known to have called himself Roberts, Gulick, Hewett, and Ridge, apparently clearing *Condor* under the latter name.

The diligent Consul, M. M. Jackson, reported the best he knew of it to Secretary Seward on September 26:

"I have the honor to inform you that the British blockade-running steamer *Condor*, which cleared from this port on the 24th instant . . . with a valuable cargo, including clothing for the Confederate Army, destined for Wilmington, is commanded by Captain (William N. W.) Hewett, late commander of the British ship of war *Rinaldo*, and still an officer in Her Majesty's service on half pay, under the assumed name of Samuel S. Ridge. (Hobart-Hampden, as Hewett, commanded *Rinaldo* when that ship carried Confederate agents Mason and Slidell to England after the notorious *Trent* affair.)

"The *Condor* is a new and superior vessel of about 300 tons, built expressly for running the blockade. She was built at Glasgow, where she is registered, and is insured by Donald McGregor, of London. She is of rakish build; very long, narrow in beam, and furnished with three low funnels and two short masts. She is of light draft and great speed. Her hull is painted very light lead color."

Acting Rear Admiral S. P. Lee, commander of the North Atlantic Blockade Squadron, was preparing to turn over his command to Rear Admiral David Porter as *Condor* steamed toward her destiny off Fort Fisher. So perhaps his concern with that—and a similar preoccupation among the officers of his command—accounted for the scarcity of details in official report of *Condor*'s end. Or perhaps Admiral Lee simply did not demand the prompt and complete reports that his successor would. Maybe the Unionists were not aware of some of the highly unusual circumstances of *Condor*'s last voyage. At any rate, one gets the impression that in its official reports the Federal Navy did not treat *Condor* with the respect she deserved.

It was, in all, a busy four or five days off New Inlet. *Niphon* had trapped *Night Hawk* on September 29, and run her aground. Then at 3:50 A.M. on Saturday, October 1, a *Niphon* lookout spotted a two-stacked side-wheeler attempting the run into New Inlet.

Acting Master Edmund Kemble quickly ordered a battery cast loose: in a brief chase *Niphon* threw five rounds at the steamer, and Kemble thought one of the shots struck home. But the runner tacked to the northeast and disappeared into the night.

Then almost instantly, at 4:00 A.M., another steamer popped into view, also bound for New Inlet, and promptly ran aground near the wreck of *Night Hawk*.

With a shuddering stop that wrenched Mrs. Greenhow from her berth, *Condor* had reached the end of her voyage.

On deck, the captain was properly furious with the Cape Fear pilot whose nervousness had hurled them onto the reef. The explanation was simple: the pilot had assumed that *Night Hawk*, looming before him in ominous darkness, was a Yankee blockader laying close to shore. To the pilot, the best course seemed to run for it toward the shore, and he called for *Condor* to swing hard to the starboard. This hasty action, hardly more than a nervous reflex, doomed the ship that was so important to the Confederacy. And it doomed Rose Greenhow, although it need not have.

As she hastily dressed in her stateroom, *Niphon* closed on the hapless *Condor*, hurling flares into the night sky. But the alert gun crews of Fort Fisher tumbled to their work and threw a barrage of big explosive shells at the Yankees, driving *Niphon* away: Acting Master Kemble would report to Captain O. S. Glisson, commander of the squadron's first division, that he would try again the next night.

On deck now, Rose Greenhow saw that *Condor* was not only aground but in the grip of a howling northeast wind as well. The once-superb ship now groaned pitifully as the storm smashed her against the bar. Shouts of ship officers and crew; white spray cascading across the deck; a few hundred yards away, the boom of mighty breakers against the beach—all combined to fill her with dread. But the threatening elements of nature were not all. Capture by the Yankees meant imprisonment, and she knew what that meant. Early in the war she had served time in Washington's mangy Old Capital Prison for espionage. Now, as a known Rebel spy, she could expect still harsher treatment if captured while trying to run the blockade. She must find Captain Hewett and tell him she must be put ashore.

First, she found two other *Condor* passengers and received their support for immediately debarking via lifeboat. They were James B. Holcombe, a Confederate diplomat, and a youthful Lieutenant Wilson. The three of them approached Captain Hewett and asked for a boat to shore.

But he assured them the situation was much less perilous than it seemed. The wind was falling, *Condor* was firmly stuck on the bottom and in no danger of cracking apart. And there was scant threat from the Yankee either, since the big guns of Fort Fisher had them well protected. Wait until daybreak, by all means, the captain said. Trying to go ashore now would be foolhardy; far more dangerous by all odds than staying aboard. He convinced Holcombe and Wilson.

But Rose persisted, fearing capture more than the mountainous waves that crashed around them in the night. She pleaded and then she raged, clutching the leather reticule that swung from her neck. She *would* be put ashore, Captain Hewett, and that was that.

Finally the British admiral agreed. He ordered the pilot—the same whose bad judgment put *Condor* on the shoal—to take a boat with two crewmen and head for shore with Mrs. Greenhow and the Confederate agents Holcombe and Wilson. Dawn was beginning to break as the tiny boat was launched in the booming combers that clutched at *Condor's* sides.

Before they were well under way, the boat slipped broadside in the waves, uncontrollable. A mountain of black-green water smashed it from the side and rolled over it, capsizing the boat and spilling its occupants into the cold Atlantic. Holcombe was swept away, later to float half-drowned to shore and survival. The other men clutched to the capsized boat and also drifted eventually to shore.

But Rebel Rose, enveloped in heavy folds of clothing, and weighted down by the heavy leather bag around her neck, sank in the churning, hissing water.

As the morning progressed, the wind receded, and Hewett came ashore with a part of his crew. They learned that Mrs. Greenhow was missing, and the beach was being searched. They did not know that she already had been found.

It happened, apparently, just as her body had been washed ashore and perhaps no longer than two hours after the *Condor* lifeboat had capsized. A lone sentry was patrolling the beach north of Mound Battery when he saw the pitiful heap of clothing that contained what was left of Mrs. Greenhow. He was a recruit, and not used to the sight of death. Slowly, gingerly, he advanced and bent over the body. His fingers probed at the leather bag, its chain still looped around her neck. He removed the chain and as he lifted the heavy bag a stream of tinkling gold spilled to the sand. British sovereigns! Maybe a hundred of them! He glanced furtively to see if he had been observed; then pocketed the coins. He tried to push the sodden remains of Mrs. Greenhow back into the sea, although he must have known the surf would push it back. Then he moved quickly away.

Soon afterward Hewett and his crew, on coming ashore, learned that Rose had failed to reach safety. The Admiral himself joined the large party of searchers that combed the shoreline around Fort Fisher. It was not he, however, but another distinguished blockade runner who found the body. He was Thomas E. Taylor, a brilliantly industrious young Englishman who—as supercargo—brought many a load of valuable goods through the blockade for the Liverpool firm he represented and partly owned. In a touch of irony, one of his few failures was the *Night Hawk*, the wrecked runner whose presence off Fort Fisher had brought *Condor* to grief.

"It was I," Taylor would write later, "who found her body on the beach at daylight and afterwards took it to Wilmington. A remarkably handsome woman she was, with features which showed much character."

The body was carried to the nearby cottage of Colonel William Lamb, the young commander of Fort Fisher, where his wife dried Rose's clothing before a pine knot fire. The body was prepared for transfer by river steamer to Wilmington and burial.

Meanwhile word spread of the identity of the victim, and it soon reached the soldier who had been first to find her. In a fit of remorse at having robbed such a great lady of the South, he ran to Colonel Lamb and confessed what he had done.

"One of the soldiers who found her body brought me a small satchel," Lamb would recall years later, "which he represented was fastened to her neck, containing one hundred sovereigns."

Colonel Lamb was anxious to scotch persistent rumors that some of Mrs. Greenhow's gold, and possibly other valuables, were misappropriated by dishonest Confederates. He termed such an idea untrue, contemptible, and unkind. Yet the fact remains that Mrs. Greenhow is known to have left England with nearly 400 gold sovereigns, amounting to nearly $2,000. This constituted a large amount of the proceeds of her book. Now granting the accuracy of Colonel Lamb's observation (after all, this thorough and dedicated man was in personal charge of all the arrangements resulting from Rose's drowning on the doorstep of his fort), a likely observation is that the large part of the English gold was lost in the surf. Because of the weight of almost 400 gold sovereigns, it is probable that Rose had some of the coins secreted on herself in other ways, such as sewing them into the lining of her voluminous clothing. She may have had another purse, or purses.

Along with the missing sovereigns were several dispatch cases that carried, one may presume, important messages for the Confederacy. Apparently they were lost when the lifeboat capsized.

Under Colonel Lamb's strict supervision, Rose's baggage that remained aboard *Condor* was brought ashore, dried out, and delivered to legal authorities in Wilmington. Rose's body was promptly carried to Wilmington, where it was on view at the Seaman Bethel building before burial with solemn Confederate ceremony at Oakdale Cemetery.

Now it was late at night on the same full day that had brought death to Mrs. Greenhow and to *Condor*.

Acting Master Edmund Kemble of U.S.S. *Niphon* was considering his plans for another try at destroying the stranded blockade-runner. At 11:40 P.M. his thoughts were interrupted by word that yet another gray steamer was coming in fast from the south, steaming for New Inlet bar. Definitely it was *Niphon*'s week for action. She gave chase, several cannon blazing, but the runner crossed her bow and safely entered the Cape Fear River.

Well, Kemble thought, let's try again for the ship on the beach; throw a few shells into her machinery, at least, so she can't be salvaged. But to his disgust as he closed on *Condor*, the Fort Fisher gunners opened with a hot and accurate barrage. Somebody on *Niphon* saw that a lookout was stationed on the beached runner, and he was signaling the gunboat's position to Fort Fisher in a highly efficient manner.

Kemble discreetly steamed away.

For the next week, wary crews from Fort Fisher offloaded a portion of *Condor*'s cargo in small boats, and by night a guard remained aboard.

On the following Friday night there occurred a Keystone Cops episode which did little credit to either side. The armed Federal tug *Aster*, with a green commander, was patrolling off New Inlet bar when she spied a blockade-runner steaming for the inlet at 11:00 p.m. *Aster* gave chase with the usual disgorging of signal flares and cannon blasts. The chase was short, however: both ships blundered onto the bar at points about 250 yards apart and near the wrecks of *Night Hawk* and *Condor*.

Aster, now stuck within the range of Fort Fisher's guns, naturally lost all interest in the blockade-runner, whose name was *Annie*. After thrashing futilely for several minutes, *Aster* dispatched a boat to another nearby U.S. tug, *Berberry*, to ask for a tow. *Berberry* arrived and connected to *Aster* with an eight-inch hawser, which snapped on the first pull. They hooked it up again: *Aster* was stuck fast and would not budge, and besides, the tide was falling. Acting Master Sam Hall of the doomed tug ordered his men transferred to *Berberry*. He remained aboard with a few hands to set fire to his ship.

Berberry then started churning for deep water, banging hard on the bottom, but still free. But after going a short distance, it was found—to the horror of her captain—that someone had forgotten to haul in the eight-inch hawser, and it was now firmly wrapped around *Berberry*'s propeller. The skipper, Acting Ensign Milton Griffith, ordered every piece of available fabric—even awnings and blankets—hoisted as jury-rigged sails. It may have looked humiliating, but it worked well enough to carry *Berberry* to safe water where she could nurse her foul propeller and sprung seams.

Back on *Aster*, Hall and his four remaining comrades got a good fire going above the magazine and scrambled for their boat. As they began rowing around one side of *Aster*'s bow, they were startled to encounter—coming around the *other* side—another longboat, containing fifteen equally surprised Englishmen: the chief engineer and fourteen firemen from the blockade-runner *Annie!*

Apparently, in the dark, the boat from *Annie* had mistaken the small boat activity around *Aster* for Confederate operations and, seeking safety, had headed for the scene. Recognizing their blunder, the English thrashed their oars wildly to reverse their direction as Hall yelled at them to come alongside. When they ignored three such commands Hall unleashed the only artillery he had aboard: a .36-caliber Colt revolver. One shot across the English boat was enough to discourage any further try at escape, and the blockade-runners followed sheepishly as the Federals rowed toward *Berberry*.

The ill-fated boat from the blockade-runner *Annie* had strayed from its fellows when it fell so limply into Union hands. *Annie*'s entire complement had in fact rushed precipitously into her boats, and all but the one whose fate we have described headed straight for *Condor*. No one has re-

corded (perhaps from sheer embarrassment) why the crew
of one stranded blockade-runner should have made straight
for another whose position was hardly better. Yet the reckless crew of *Annie* did this and, for their pains, were met
with a ferocious if inaccurate hail of small arms fire from
the Rebel guard aboard *Condor*.

"Yankees," the Rebs hollered, "Yankees! Let 'em have it!
They're coming in to burn us!"

As the misidentified Britons reeled off in the direction of
shore, the fire set aboard stranded *Aster* by her captain finally burst through the superstructure and flared across the
water. It was now 2:40 A.M.

Ashore at Fort Fisher's Mound Battery, Confederate artillerymen were bewildered by the variety of action trans-
piring out beyond the breakers. A ship was afire. Muskets
and pistols popped and crackled. Men were yelling and
cursing as small boats shuttled everywhere. The artillerymen responded in the only way they knew. They hurled a
barrage of shells out into the pandemonium on the bar.

Not a shot struck anything.

The *Annie*'s crew (except for the one unlucky boatload)
struggled ashore, glad to be rid of the whole sticky business.
Dawn would hardly break before the blockading squadron's
officers would start to bicker over why nobody had thought
to board *Annie* and set her afire. The chance, once missed,
was gone forever. On the next high tide a Confederate crew
got *Annie* off the bar and she steamed neatly into the Cape
Fear River.

As more days passed, a portion of *Condor*'s cargo was
tediously offloaded. But it was slow going and the weather
complicated matters. The ship was breaking up rapidly
now.

Emerging from the mists that envelop the fate of the bulk
of her cargo is one poignant entry in the diary of Colonel
Lamb of Fort Fisher. On December 4, he recorded:

"We received a lot of toys, etc., sent by Captain Hewett, of the *Condor* . . ."

As events hurtled on toward the Unionists' first attack on Fort Fisher, a letter from General Whiting to Colonel Lamb on December 23 asked if Lamb would keep a lookout on *Condor*'s wreck to watch for the expected invasion. He was, said Whiting, "more afraid of that way of attack than any other."

Lamb replied by telegram the same day: "A lookout cannot stay on *Condor* at high tide."

The war was over for the slim three-stacked steamer, whose first and last voyage had begun with such bright hope. And the cold rains of the Confederacy's last winter dripped through the Spanish moss of Oakdale Cemetery on the fresh grave of the *Condor* affair's only victim: the courageous Rebel Rose.

Hobart-Hampden, alias Hewett, alias Ridge, etc., would go on to more adventures and die in 1886, rich in years and in honors as Admiral-in-Chief of the Ottoman Empire's Navy and Vice Admiral, R.N., Ret. Upon his death the London *Daily Telegraph* eulogized him in a special editorial:

"Altogether Augustus Charles Hobart was a remarkable man—bluff, bold, dashing, and somewhat dogged. . . . It would be unjust to sneer at Hobart as a mercenary. He was no more a hired sword than were the blades of Schomberg and Berwick, of Maurice de Saxe and Eugene of Savoy. When there was fighting to be done Hobart liked to be in it—that is all. Of the fearless, dashing, adventurous Englishmen, ready to go anywhere and do anything, Hobart was a brilliantly representative type."

CHAPTER 5

"'Tween th' Devil and th' Deep Blue Sea!"

The story of the *Night Hawk* is one of the most thrilling of all blockade-runner tales. It reflects the reckless daring and ingenuity that was characteristic of the men who ran the gauntlet.

Thomas E. Taylor was one of these men. *Night Hawk* was one of the many blockade-runners aboard which he sailed as supercargo. While in his early twenties, Tom Taylor not only managed the business affairs of vessels belonging to a large British export house, he made *sure* the cargoes reached their destinations by sailing aboard the blockade-runners owned by his firm. Without any question he was one of the most successful men to ever run the blockade of the Confederate States.

He was a bold and dashing specimen of a man. Although barely out of his teens, he probably made more money than anyone his age in the entire Confederacy.

Tom Taylor was a traveling man, too, and well versed in the ways of the world. He knew also the ways of worldly women. They flocked around him as if there were no other men in town. And he liked the attention.

He realized that each trip through the blockade might be his last, so why not live a little? The world was his for the asking. He had nothing to lose but his life. And a night on the town cost only $350 in Confederate notes.

Thirty-five years later he set down his personal narrative of "Adventures, Risks, and Escapes during the American Civil War." His book, long out of print, is entitled *Running the Blockade*, and was published in London by John Murray in 1896. Tom Taylor made twenty-eight successful trips through the Yankee barricade, "and considering the narrow squeaks that I had, and that I only came to grief once in the *Night Hawk*, I had a great deal to be thankful for."

The *Night Hawk* was a perfect specimen of a blockade-runner. She was a side-wheel steamer of 600 tons, long and low, schooner-rigged fore and aft with two smokestacks. Her length was 220 feet; her beam measured 21 feet 6 inches; and she drew 11 feet of water. She had been launched at Prestwick, England, and brought to Liverpool for engine installation. Her total construction cost had been 30,000 pounds.

Tom Taylor had been looking forward to sailing aboard the *Night Hawk*. She was one of the speedy and elusive fleet of vessels built expressly for running the blockade. In fact, she had been built according to his personal recommendations. Her costly specifications were designed in terms of speed and daring. Her crew was a reckless, but capable bunch. Many of them were here today gone tomorrow. But the profit *Night Hawk* would earn, if she made two successful trips, was worth all the expense and trouble.

Following her maiden voyage from England to Bermuda, she sailed for the Confederacy on September 26, 1864. Her cargo consisted of a great quantity of "provisions" for the Rebel army, twenty-six bags of saltpeter, sixty pigs of lead, and miscellaneous "hardware."

Leaving Hamilton Harbour, Bermuda, the *Night Hawk* had hardly gotten under way when she ran aground and hung for several hours on a coral ledge within sight of the harbor. Fortunately, though, the vessel came off without damage and proceeded on her journey.

The destiny of the voyage was summed up early in the trip by Taylor in his memoirs: ". . . the Wilmington pilot was quite unknown to me, and I could see from the outset that he was very nervous and badly wanting in confidence."

They had sighted unusually few patrolling warships. However, on the third night as the blockade-runner approached the entrance to Wilmington, they found themselves uncomfortably near a large blockader. The alert cruiser did not hesitate to greet the *Night Hawk* and her crew with a quick broadside.

Nevertheless, the resolute runner pushed her bow in the direction of New Inlet and began zigzagging through the Yankee dragnet. She received a brusque round of fire but managed somehow to get well within the Union fleet.

However, luck was not with her. It was not long before the *Night Hawk* encountered the U.S.S. *Niphon,* one of the fast, new warships that already had captured more than her share of blockade-runners. The *Niphon* fired repeatedly into the *Night Hawk,* four shots of which pierced the blockade-runner's hull. At that point, Fort Fisher entered the action as if to offer encouragement to the troubled fugitive. Three of the nearest batteries on land roared defiance, and the Confederates fired a rocket into the air trying to confuse the blockading fleet.

In a diversionary move, *Night Hawk* "showed her lights," which caused the U.S.S. *Niphon* to think she was surrendering. Then, when the warship let down her guard, the blockade-runner rang up full steam and "streaked southeast almost out of sight."

But the chase was not over yet. Having arrived in the

vicinity of the bar, over which they must pass to clear the inlet, they encountered two Federal launches lying directly in their path.

It was almost midnight, and according to Tom Taylor, the tide was dead low. He pleaded with the pilot not to try to enter, and suggested heading for the open sea. The pilot, though, was "so demoralized by the firing we had gone through and the nearness of the launches, which were constantly throwing up rockets, that he insisted on putting her at the Bar."

As Tom Taylor predicted, the *Night Hawk* ran fast aground. With the tide against her, she quickly broached broadside to the breakers, which began pounding her. But she was only about a half mile from Fort Fisher and there was still hope.

"We kept our engines going for some time—but to no purpose as we found we were only being forced by the tide more on to the breakers."

By then the pursuing *Niphon* had spotted the stranded runner, and Union cutters were approaching under a continuous round of fire. As the old quartermaster of the *Night Hawk* put it, "They were truly 'tween th' devil and th' deep blue sea!"

The next thing Tom Taylor remembers was the great confusion and panic that prevailed among the pilot and crew as the Federal launches came alongside. "The pilot and signalman rushed to the dinghy, lowered it, and made good their escape; the captain lost his head and disappeared. . . . When the Northerners jumped on board they were terribly excited. I don't know whether they expected resistance or not, but they acted more like maniacs than sane men, firing their revolvers and cutting right and left with their cutlasses."

Tom Taylor had faced the possibility of capture before. But at this moment he must have felt that the likelihood of escape was just about impossible. Throwing overboard a bag of private dispatches, he stepped forward on the poop and surrendered.

"Oh, you surrender, do you?" came the Yankee's reply (accompanied, Taylor recalls, by the choicest oaths upon his parentage). Whereupon the Unionist fired two shots in Tom Taylor's face.

"It was a miracle he did not kill me," Taylor recalled, "I heard the bullets whiz past my head."

Unable to float the *Night Hawk* off the shoal, the Yankees looted the vessel and set the ship on fire. She began to blaze fiercely.

"At this moment," says Taylor, "one of our firemen, an Irishman, sung out, 'Begorra, we shall all be in the air in a minute, the ship is full of gunpowder!'

"No sooner did the Northern sailors hear this than a panic seized them, and they rushed to their boats, threatening to leave their officers behind if they did not come along."

To Tom Taylor's delight the Yankees dropped him like "a hot potato" and rowed off into the night, taking the crew of the blockade-runner as prisoners with the exception of the second officer, an engineer, four seamen, and Taylor.

Since the *Night Hawk* was wrapped in a sheet of flame there was no alternative but to try to reach shore by whatever means available.

"We chuckled at our lucky escape, but we were not out of the woods yet, as we had only a boat half stove in, in which to reach the shore through some 300 yards of surf, and we were afraid at any moment that our enemies finding there was no powder on board might return. . . ."

Once they reached the beach, the survivors of the *Night Hawk* were greeted by Confederate soldiers who had been watching from shore the episode beyond the breakers. They administered to the needs of the exhausted mariners, and then several boatloads of volunteers headed for the burning ship to try to extinguish the flames. After hours of determined effort the fire was put out. But much of the hull and superstructure of the brand new runner was completely charred. The possibility of saving her seemed almost hopeless.

However, with the help of Colonel Lamb at Fort Fisher, who sent some three hundred Negroes to assist in bailing, hope of bringing *Night Hawk* to port in one piece brightened. Also, another of Taylor's ships, *Banshee II*, had just reached Wilmington, and her crew offered a hand at freeing the immovable blockade-runner.

But it was not at all an easy task. The Union prize crew that fled the *Night Hawk* the evening before most certainly lost a few points with their commanding officer. They wanted revenge, and they intended to get it. Every day the entire fleet of gunboats shelled the workers aboard the *Night Hawk*, and at night the Federals became bolder. Boat after boat of marines were sent in hoping to recapture the stricken blockade-runner.

Tom Taylor needed only to complain to his friend Colonel Lamb of Fort Fisher, "who put a stop to the annoyance by lending a couple of companies to defend us, and one night, when our enemies rowed close up with the intention of boarding us, they were glad to sheer off with the loss of a lieutenant and several men."

It was not so much the determined efforts of the Confederates, but the misfortune of another blockade-runner that was to prove to be *Night Hawk*'s salvation. After struggling for a week without budging the grounded vessel, the blockade-runner *Condor* came in on the dark tide of October 1, 1864. Thinking the stranded *Night Hawk* to be a Union blockader at anchor, *Condor*'s pilot tried to veer off to avoid her and, in doing so, ran afoul of the same shoal that had caused *Night Hawk* so much grief.

"It is an ill wind that blows nobody good," Taylor wrote. "But now we had a hold for our chain cables by making them fast to the wreck (*Condor*), and were able gradually to haul her off a little during each tide. . . . On the seventh day we had her afloat in a gut between the bank and the shore, and at high water we steamed under our own steam gaily up the river to Wilmington."

The *Night Hawk* was almost a complete wreck. A great amount of money was spent in making her seaworthy. "Her sides were all corrugated with the heat, and her stern so twisted that her starboard quarter was some two feet higher than her port one, and not a particle of woodwork was left unconsumed."

After extensive repairs, the *Night Hawk* left Wilmington with a valuable cargo and successfully ran the blockade, ". . . which made her pay, notwithstanding all her bad luck and the amount spent upon her."

CHAPTER 6

Ella Sank and Richmond Fell

Less than two months remained before the tightening noose of the Yankee blockade would strangle the sea roads to Wilmington. The Confederacy was dying that December of 1864, but it was dying hard, and the life that remained was nourished by that peculiar blend of patriotism and greed that kept the slim white steamers racing into Wilmington.

By this time, the chased and the chasers had refined the game to a stylized perfection, a form as rigid as the fox and the hounds, with all its subtleties. Each side was well equipped and knew what it was doing. Take, for example, Lieutenant Commander D. L. Braine, captain of the *Pequot*.

Braine had the 593-ton gunboat close off the South Carolina coast at early afternoon on December 2. *Pequot* was on inshore patrol, lying in the path of runners that would steam up the coast, waiting for the moonless dark and rising tide that would ease their passage through the inshore blockaders that clustered around Old Inlet. It was accepted blockade-running practice to make landfall either north or south of Cape Fear at some hopefully deserted stretch of coast lying against the silhouette-concealing dunes, then to run for the river entrance when conditions were right.

Braine was in luck that Saturday afternoon.

The runner was coming from the south, heading for shore at Little River Inlet on the North Carolina line, when the lookout spotted her at 1:00 P.M. For forty minutes Braine held *Pequot* motionless, hard to see against the shore from the incoming vessel. When the runner had almost reached the inlet she bore northeast, hugging the shoreline, pulling away from *Pequot*. Braine rang for full speed and the chase was on.

Churning eastward, the captain's plan was to intercept the runner and crowd her into shore. But the runner's lookout had spotted *Pequot*, and now the long, lead-colored two-stacker had the wind up and changed course toward the east herself, her giant thrashing paddles pulling her ahead of the screw-propelled gunboat.

Soon another change: the blockade runner veered to the southeast, back toward open ocean, as the dogged Captain Braine began firing signal guns to call other cruisers to the chase. He yelled to the engine room for black smoke, another signal, but no warship came. The two ships plunged on into the afternoon.

Braine still had the runner well in sight after more than four hours of pursuit, and at 6:00 P.M. the fugitive had reached the end of Frying Pan Shoals, a twenty-mile finger of submerged sand trailing southeast into the Atlantic from Cape Fear. Abruptly the side-wheeler spun around and steered northwest along the shoal, back toward the Cape and Old Inlet. Braine hauled *Pequot* around and followed as best he could as the ghostly vessel disappeared into darkness.

At 8:20 P.M. the cruiser captain sent up a final cluster of signal flares to alert the inshore blockading squadron, pulled offshore to safe water, and patrolled slowly for the night's duration. The runner had eluded them, yet Braine and the 130-man *Pequot* crew had succeeded perhaps better than they realized in their stubborn, sixty-mile chase after a steamer whose name they didn't know. They would know it soon enough.

She was the *Ella*.

As the blockade-runner glided through the chill December night, threading past the dim shapes of Federal cruisers, sounding constantly to keep clear of Frying Pan Shoals, her captain and crew had little time to curse their miserable luck. They were more than four days out of Nassau; by now they should have been safely inside Old Channel Bar, steaming for Wilmington under the friendly guns of Fort Caswell. Instead they were trapped between the blockading fleet and Cape Fear itself. The heavy December mists helped screen *Ella* from the fleet, yet increased the peril of blundering into an unseen cruiser, or running aground. Hours passed.

By 5:00 A.M. *Ella*'s plight was desperate. It would be hopeless if daybreak found her still outside the western bar channel. She was now near Bald Head Point and the Confederate battery at Fort Holmes, and the pilot had one last chance to bring her home: he rang for steam and steered for the bar.

It was a lookout aboard U.S.S. *Emma* who saw her first.

The cruiser was patrolling in 3½ fathoms (21 feet) along the western bar. She jumped to full speed and neatly blocked *Ella*'s path, firing a signal rocket to alarm the fleet. The small screw steamer *Emma*, light at 350 tons, only mounted eight guns. She opened with a broadside as best she could but missed at a 700-yard range, then steered directly for *Ella* as the runner pivoted in a last wild dash for sanctuary. The cruiser's leadsman called out a dangerously shallow draft, 2½ fathoms: the blockade-runner was 500 yards farther inshore, but Acting Lieutenant Thomas Dunn wouldn't risk pushing his gunboat closer to the booming surf. There was no need to. Even as he ordered *Emma*'s

engines shut down, he could see the big side-wheeler was
hard aground off Smith's Island.

Alerted by Federal signaling and activity in the fleet
throughout the night, the Confederates at little Fort Holmes
had anxiously awaited developments. Now, as a pale dawn
tinted the heavy mists off Bald Head Point, they saw *Ella*
for the first time. She signaled frantically. Colonel John
Hedrick, commanding Fort Holmes, knew his limitations.
He dashed off a telegram to General Hebert at Smithville,
six miles away:

"Steamer *Ella* is ashore about 1⅓ miles off; draft 6 feet.
If she can be lightened before day the ship can be saved.
Can you send a steamboat over? She wants a guard. I have
refused. Shall I comply? If you send small boats they will
be of service. Let them report here and I will have a pilot
ready."

Colonel Hedrick's rather hand-wringing telegram did
not reach General Hebert. The general, unknown to Hedrick, already had scented action and was on his way to Bald
Head to have a look at things for himself when the wire
reached his headquarters at Smithville. Captain Hardeman
answered it.

"Use your discretion about sending a guard. Can send
you no boats. No steamer can be had."

It was still just a few minutes past 6:00 A.M.

Back on *Emma*, only 500 yards away from the stranded
runner, Captain Dunn told his executive officer to lower a
boat, take an armed crew, and board *Ella* and set her on
fire "at all hazards." *Emma*'s gun crew plugged away meanwhile with the cruiser's four modest port guns.

Daybreak was coming fast now and the Rebel shore gunners were ready. Hardly had the launch from *Emma* hit the
water than the Fort Holmes crews unleashed a withering
fire. Evidently the "hazards" were greater than Captain
Dunn had thought possible; he hastily recalled the boat and

hoisted it aboard at 6:30 A.M. At least six boats now could be observed in the roiling water around *Ella*. The Confederates would fight gamely to save the crew and salvage the cargo. Cannon blazed from the sand dunes. For the moment, Captain Dunn decided he and *Emma* had done all they could for the Union cause. He steered a course away from the shore guns' range.

General Hebert watched it all from the dunes, and took the play away from Colonel Hedrick. He sent a telegram back to his Smithville headquarters, to Hardeman, who had refused Hedrick any help: "Send a steamer here to take off crew of *Ella*."

Captain Dunn, meanwhile, returned to the fleet and signaled to Lieutenant-Commander George Young on the U.S.S. *Maratanza*, senior officer in the area.

Young ordered gunboats *Britannia*, *Aries*, *Huron*, and *Chippewa* to run in and try the range; he wanted to make sure *Ella* was thoroughly disabled to avoid any chance of the Rebels refloating her. The cruisers made one tentative pass but were discouraged by fire from the shore batteries, particularly a 100-pounder Brooke rifle, which found them in easy range. Young signaled the ships to pull back at long range and fire from fixed positions.

Meanwhile, the indefatigable Lieutenant Braine steamed up in *Pequot* and joined *Britannia* and *Aries*. Braine indeed was *Ella*'s nemesis. On his second or third broadside, missles from *Pequot* struck the runner's boilers, and they exploded like a clap of doom. *Ella* would move no more. Watching in satisfaction from *Maratanza*, Lieutenant-Commander Young estimated that *Ella* was struck some forty times in the fusillade.

Ella's fate was even plainer from the shore. At 10:00 A.M., General Hebert dispatched a telegram to General Whiting in Wilmington: "The *Ella* is ashore 1½ miles from shore, opposite the Hill battery or left of land fronts. She is abandoned. We keep the enemy far off, but their shots reach the ship. She has been struck. She can't be saved."

One hour later Hebert reported again to the Wilmington commander: "The *Ella* is hulled and full of water. She is lost. The enemy has reached with his shot to Colonel Hedrick's house. He is still firing slowly."

Young now plotted an expedition to board *Ella* and set her afire that night. He stopped the bombardment, but posted enough lookouts and armament within range of the stranded runner to prevent the Confederates from salvaging her. The day dragged on under leaden skies.

Young's plan was to send in *Britannia, Tristram Shandy,* and *Nansemond* as close as practicable, blazing away to scatter any Confederates who might have sneaked back to the vessel after dark. Then cruisers would be trailed by several small boats carrying seamen who would board and burn the runner. At exactly 9:30 P.M., the expedition began in almost total darkness. That, in fact, was the chief trouble. They couldn't find *Ella.* Moreover, the wind was rising, and mist swirled over the shoal-ridden coastline. Word came for the cruisers to abandon the proposed attack and return to their regular night stations.

The expedition was commanded by Acting Volunteer Lieutenant Samuel Huse, captain of *Britannia.* After ordering the cruisers to haul off to deeper water, he went back in toward shore in his gig, as far as the breakers, but because of the heavy weather could find no sign of *Ella.* He returned to his ship and instructed all the cruisers to pull still further offshore to their regular night duty stations.

The behavior of Acting Volunteer Lieutenant Edward Devens, commanding *Tristram Shandy,* therefore seems extraordinarily eager. Devens did not haul off with the rest of the squadron. Instead, the 444-ton gunboat hovered all night in the bar-infested, mist-covered water around Marshall Shoal. The depth ranged from 2¼ to 3 fathoms, only 13 to 18 feet.

At 2:00 A.M. Devens and the *Shandy* crew had a moment of excitement as a small steam launch was sighted in the breakers toward Smith's Island. *Shandy* challenged the cutter and received no reply. The apparent Confederate turned to shore and disappeared in the mist.

Now it was 5:00 A.M. and Devens made ready to be the first Unionist to resume the attack on helpless *Ella* as dawn broke for Sunday, December 4. He eased the cruiser toward the spot where all reckoning said the runner had to lay. At 6:10, with his ship in only 15 feet of water, the mists lifted slightly and there was *Ella*, not more than 60 yards away.

Shandy's gun crew had little to tax their marksmanship. *Ella*, large for her breed at more than 1000 tons, lay high on the shoal, listing to port, her stern raised and her head in the breakers. The Union gunners hurled percussion shells into her at point-blank range as fast as they could reload.

Minutes later there was enough daylight for the Fort Holmes gunners to make out the Federal cruiser so irritatingly close to the crippled runner. Perhaps some of them recognized *Shandy* as a vessel that once had been on their side. She was a captured blockade-runner, converted to a gunboat by the Yankees.

There was little wind that morning, and the crafty Devens capitalized on the dense fog of white smoke as his guns puffed over the water. By careful seamanship he eased *Shandy* along behind the almost-opaque smoke cloud and effectively camouflaged his vessel. The Confederates threw a hot fire from a variety of shore batteries, and geysers squirted everywhere around *Shandy*, but she was not struck.

At 7:00 A.M. Devens decided his luck had been pushed far enough. He withdrew seaward, carefully tabulating his expended ammunition: 29 twelve-pounder shells and 13 twenty-pounder shells. He also turned in a totally wrong report as to the circumstances of *Ella*'s last cruise.

"I am very certain," he told Lieutenant-Commander Young, "she is cotton loaded and was running out by the Marshall Shoal channel."

After *Shandy*'s orgy of shelling, the Federal chieftains apparently were satisfied that the blockade-runner wasn't going anywhere. They called off the fleet bombardment, and for the rest of that Sunday were content to keep a sharp lookout that no Confederate salvagers approached the ship. With the cruisers watchful, and the weather heavy, the Rebels had little stomach for any attempt to unload the runner.

Monday dawned cold and misty. Aboard *Maratanza*, Lieutenant-Commander Young conferred with Lieutenant Dunn of *Emma*. They agreed that a boarding party must be attempted again to set fire to *Ella* and assure the destruction of her cargo. But instead of sending another unwieldy, and easily spotted, armada of small boats, they decided to send in only one boat. Acting Ensign Isaac S. Sampson of *Emma* was placed in charge of the dangerous solo mission. The plans were completed as Monday dragged on.

It was not until 1:30 A.M. of Tuesday, December 6, that tide and weather conditions were right for Sampson and his picked crew to drop one of *Emma*'s boats and pull toward shore with muffled oars. There was one other officer: Acting Third Assistant Engineer A. L. Churchill. The crew of six comprised James Green, Charles Miller, Peter Hans, William Scott, Joseph Fitzpatrick, and Charles Chapman.

Sampson steered a course directly toward Bald Head Light. The water grew shallow as they crossed Marshall Shoal, and with a reading of only seven feet Sampson saw the runner looming up through the darkness. Soon they glided up under *Ella*'s port bow, which faced offshore.

On the beach 250 yards away Confederate sentries droned their orders. Sampson and his men could hear them clearly. But no one had spotted them, and they could see no sign of life aboard the derelict. Sampson detailed two men to guard the boat while he and the other five scrambled up *Ella*'s iron-plated sides. They were armed with pistols and cutlasses, and they carried jugs of kerosene.

With Sampson leading the way, the five Federals padded aft on the runner's shattered deck. They came first to the pilothouse: the young officer poked his dark lantern inside, then moved quickly on. Next was the ship's galley and adjoining storeroom. Here they sloshed kerosene on anything that looked combustible and then moved still farther aft, to a cabin over the ship's two powerful oscillating engines, and repeated the process. The next to be doused with kerosene was a messroom. Picking their way through heavy boxes and barrels which jammed the deck they reached the captain's cabin.

Signs of the skipper's hasty departure were plain in his handsome quarters, which lay in total disarray. Sampson searched hurriedly and learned, for the first time, the name of the vessel that had occupied the fleet's energies for more than three days. He established from a cargo receipt that *Ella* had been loaded at Nassau.

The Union men poked stealthily about the ship for a few more anxious minutes, wondering when the Rebel batteries at Fort Holmes might open fire. They broke open a case of good Enfield rifles and lowered seven of them into their launch. Another useful souvenir was the ship's compass, which they took, but that was all.

Sampson peered into the hold, carefully releasing a small ray of light from the dark lantern. He saw that the ship was half-filled with water; there was no way to inspect the hold cargo.

From *Emma* the young lieutenant had brought several

After seeing all hope of escape impossible many blockade-running captains would beach their vessels in a do-or-die effort to reach shore safely and land valuable cargo.

Franklin D. Roosevelt Library

The blockade-runner *Margaret and Jessie* made eighteen successful trips between the Confederacy and neutral ports before being captured while attempting to enter Wilmington, North Carolina. She was converted to a gunboat, named the *Gettysburg,* and in the hands of Union officials later was successful in capturing other blockade-runners. BELOW: A crate of Austrian rifles is brought ashore from the sunken blockade-runner *Ranger* off Holden Beach, North Carolina. Bayonets, still in their leather scabbards, are stacked neatly inside.

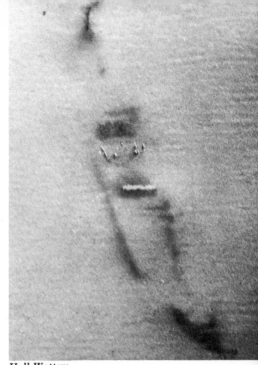

RIGHT: From an altitude of 600 feet the outline of the sunken blockade-runner *Ranger* is clearly visible. BELOW: Hall Watters perches atop lead ingots salvaged from the blockade-runner *Phantom* 100 years after the ship sank off New Topsail inlet, North Carolina. Musket stocks were retrieved from the *Ranger*.

Hall Watters

Dave Horner

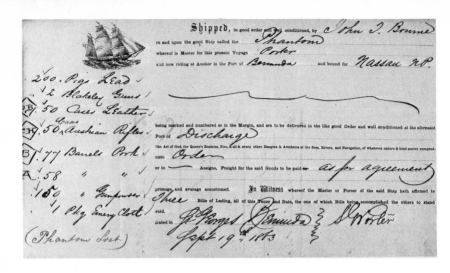

200 Pigs Lead
2 Blakeley Guns
50 Cases Leather
50 Cans Austrian Rifles
77 Barrels Pork
58 " "
150 " Gunpowder
1 Pkg Emery Cloth
(*Phantom Lost*)

Original cargo manifest of Confederate blockade-runner *Phantom* bearing the signature of her captain, S. G. Porter, and listing cargo destined for the Confederate States of America. A penciled notation at the bottom left corner was made after it was learned the *Phantom* had been lost. BELOW: Brass railroad padlocks encrusted with calciferous marine life were brought up from the *Ella* after a century on the bottom.

Hall Watters

Jim Wamsley

The author displays 100-year-old beam from the famous blockade-runner *Ella*. The ship was stranded on Marshall Shoal near Cape Fear and became a total wreck. Her loss was a disaster for the Confederacy as the vessel carried an extremely valuable cargo intended for the troops of General Robert E. Lee.

Dave Horner

A diver studies the whirlpool of surging sea around the 100-year-old shipwreck of a blockade-runner. BELOW: The "gray ghost" *Aries* was captured off Bull Bay, South Carolina while trying to reach Charleston with munitions of war.

Henry B. du Pont

Blockade-runners crowd St. George's Harbour, Bermuda. BELOW: Artist's conception of the *Mary Celeste* sinking off Gibb's Hill Lighthouse.

LEFT: "If you choose to, you can descend some eighty feet beneath uncertain green water and comb through the remains of the *Mary Celeste.* If you look sharply you'll see the muskets she was carrying to the Confederate States." RIGHT: On the bottom off Bermuda, Harry Cox (left) and Pete Clark cling to the paddle-wheel of the once proud *Mary Celeste.*

Blockade-runners like the *Hope* were fast, sleek vessels. This one was built in England in 1864 for the Confederate Government. She was captured after a few runs, off Cape Fear. BELOW: The U. S. S. *Connecticut* was one of the fastest and most feared blockading Union warships.

The U. S. S. *Peterhoff*, before she became a monument beneath the sea.

One of the cannon recovered from the sunken wreck of the U. S. S. *Peterhoff*. BELOW: There might be a chest of gold in the wreck of the blockade-runner *Beauregard* off Carolina Beach, North Carolina, but strong currents and shifting sands have protected it thus far.

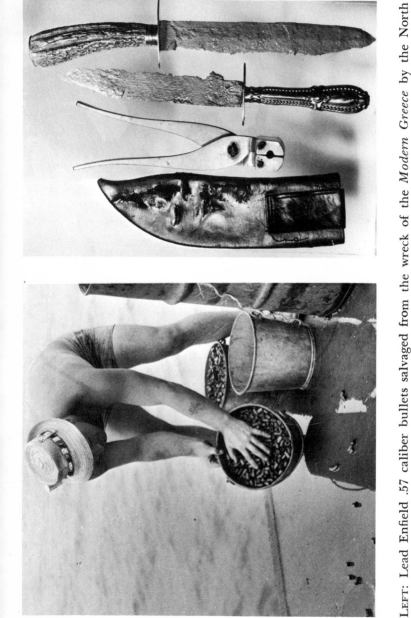

LEFT: Lead Enfield .57 caliber bullets salvaged from the wreck of the *Modern Greece* by the North Carolina Department of Archives and History. RIGHT: Bowie knives, bullet mold, and leather sheath represent some of the artifacts recovered from the sunken *Modern Greece*.

From the *Modern Greece*, thirty-five feet down, a diver wrestles an encrusted relic to the surface.

Phil Morgan

Phil Morgan

Scuba divers have found the anchor of the *Fanny and Jenny* but the gold and jewel-studded sword for General R. E. Lee still remains hidden beneath shifting sands.

After being cleaned and polished the padlocks make handsome souvenirs. Their spring-lock mechanism still functions perfectly. BELOW: Lead bars, muskets, and other articles recovered by the author from several wrecked blockade-runners.

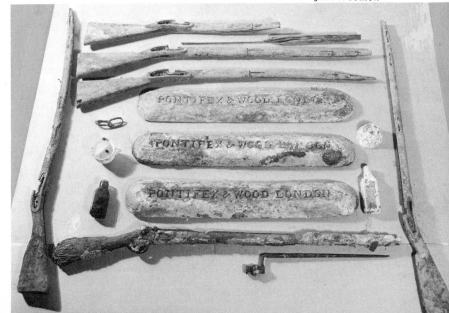

Paul J. Tzimoulis

Dave Horner

LEFT: Festooned with tawny sea whips and purple plumes an ancient anchor marks the underwater grave of a long lost blockade-runner. RIGHT: A diver searches the sea floor around the anchor of the blockade-runner *Kate.*

24-pound howitzer shells with short train fuses already cut
and inserted. Now he ordered his crew to pass them aboard
and place them in critical locations close to the engines.

Sampson ordered all but Churchill (a munitions expert)
and one crewman to return to the launch. Then, moving
swiftly, he and Churchill lit fires at the four areas they had
doused with kerosene. Flames licked through the galley, the
messroom, the engine room, and the captain's cabin. The
three Unionists scrambled back into their boat where the
crewmen were ready to pull for safe water and their gunboat. As their oars bit into the sea, red flashes erupted from
the guns of Fort Holmes as the Rebel artillerymen realized
what the raiders had done.

Briefly, the flames of burning *Ella* lit the straining faces
of the Union sailors as geysers from Confederate shells
hissed in the water. But then the night closed over them
and with it came safety. Minutes later, they were back
aboard *Emma*, at 4:30 A.M., in time to hear the muffled
crump-crump of the howitzer shells exploding in the machinery of the blockade runner.

Ella burned fiercely for three hours. In his pleased report
to Admiral Porter, Lieutenant-Commander Young gloated
over the expedition's success. He also reported a large number of floating boxes in the general area which apparently
had been thrown off *Ella*'s decks in a frantic attempt to
lighten her when she first ran aground. The boxes, marked
with the letters "L.C." inside a triangle and the figure "18,"
contained 5½-inch rifle shells. Young added that there
wasn't the slightest chance of the Rebels getting anything
worthwhile off *Ella* now: a small amount of cargo, perhaps,
but in damaged condition.

Sampson would comment later that *Ella* was a new
steamer (he was almost right; she had been new in September, and this apparently was her third voyage), and he

judged that the iron-hulled side-wheeler sporting two iron masts and two funnels was above 1000 tons burden.

One old Cape Fear pilot recalled years later that *Ella* had belonged to the Bee Company of Charleston, and that on her fateful voyage she carried "a large and valuable cargo almost entirely owned by private parties and speculators." *

There was plenty of Confederate government cargo on board, however. In a six weeks' report for the period ending December 6, 1864, Colonel T. L. Bayne, Chief of the Bureau of Foreign Supplies of the Confederate War Department, listed *Ella*'s government account cargo as 1 case of bismuth, 147 barrels of pork, 40 tierces of beef, 30 packages of horseshoe nails, 1 lifeboat, 225 sacks of coffee, 1 case of spool cotton, and 23 cases of Enfield rifles.

There is a story in James Sprunt's *Cape Fear Chronicles* which says one group of Confederates on Bald Head actually succeeded in boarding *Ella* at some point during the Yankee fusillade before she was burned. In Sprunt's brief account, men from an Edenton, North Carolina, battery boarded her and unloaded some cargo even as Federal shells crashed into *Ella*'s hulk.

Undoubtedly a wrecked blockade-runner, even partially salvageable, was a demoralizing affair for the deprived Rebel garrisons close by. There is no doubt that drunkenness and black marketeering flourished when cargoes were brought hastily ashore. Obviously Mr. Sprunt meant to illustrate this when he went on to say that "for a month afterward nearly the whole garrison were on 'a tight,'" yet that surely must have been an exaggeration. Sprunt even implies

---

* William C. Bee was one of the organizers of the Importing and Exporting Company of South Carolina, which was commonly referred to as "the Bee Company" because of the extremely able and patriotic leadership which William Bee provided. His was undoubtedly one of the most profitable operations engaged in the blockade-running business, and the company gained a great deal of praise from loyal Southerners because of consistent efforts to keep their privately owned cargoes out of the hands of black market speculators.

that the fort chaplain had a snootful of gin from *Ella*, and "said some very queer graces at the headquarters mess table."

What probably happened is that a furtive group of Rebels did board her during the first or second night she was aground and before she was fired by Sampson's crew. They removed some light and quickly salvageable items that included gourmet groceries and a quantity of the chaplain's London gargle. But, as is plain from Sampson's account, the great bulk of *Ella's* cargo was left aboard, part of it to be destroyed by the fire, the rest—already submerged in the hold—to be covered by settling debris as the destruction was complete.

As the Confederacy raced toward disaster that winter of 1864–1865, *Ella* was soon forgotten in the feverish last days of the blockade-running epoch along Cape Fear. Few were interested in a cargo of ruined perishables and rusting military goods. Green water surged and closed over *Ella's* bones as they drifted deeper into the sand of Marshall Shoal.

The Yankees closed up the Cape Fear and Wilmington fell, and the blockaders steamed away. In time, only a few would remember; old men in Providence who still could hear the boom of *Shandy's* broadsides; old men in Liverpool whose feet recalled the smooth new decks of a ship named *Ella*.

Finally there would be none to call her name.

ELLA–1964

Robert Watters was replacing the muffler on his Piper when Jim Wamsley and I arrived at the hangar in Wilmington at 7:00 A.M. The old muffler leaked carbon monoxide into the cockpit and made him drowsy, a highly unsanitary condition for a solo-flying fish spotter.

I helped Robert install the new muffler while Jim wandered in amazement through the hangar. It was his first trip to Cape Fear, and Robert and I were amused by his land-lubber's interest in the nautical equipment and relics that lay everywhere. He wanted to be a diver. Well, this was a good place for him to begin.

There was at least one major addition to the hangar's relic collection since my last visit: a four-foot-high pile of lead pigs, stacked like small railroad ties. I was familiar with the dull-gray, elongated chunks from the *Phantom* dive, but most of these were of a slightly different shape. They bore the legend, "Newton Keates and Company, Liverpool." I asked Robert about them; he said they had come from divers on *Modern Greece*. Even at scrap prices, I thought, this much lead should bring a fair return in salvage. And with this quantity brought from the bottom with relative ease, the amount of blockade lead still off Cape Fear must be staggering.

While I amused myself with mental calculations on the possibility of growing rich by selling antique lead, Robert Watters concluded his muffler job and Jim discovered a strange sort of relic in a clump of weeds outside the hangar: the shattered, twisted wreckage of a big airliner. He crawled inside the cockpit's remains and peered out through the smashed windshield, hands on the controls, wondering per-haps about the last thoughts of the pilot. Robert told us the plane had been the National DC-6 which crashed several years before, not far from Wilmington, killing all aboard and gaining a bizarre notoriety we well remembered. It was thought that a New York attorney aboard the plane had blown it up and sent a multitude of persons to their deaths. After the crash the Federal Aviation Agency had reassem-bled the pieces in one side of the Watters' hangar for their investigation; then they dumped it all outside in a pathetic heap, where it remained for some time.

But Jim's interest returned quickly to more ancient wrecks and relics when Hall Watters landed, taxied his

Piper to the hangar, and announced that he had just dropped
a marker on *Ella.* He had been spotting menhaden since
daybreak off the Cape Fear mouth. On his way back to
Wilmington, he scanned Marshall Shoal for our target of
the day's expedition, and there she was, plainly outlined in
the greenish-black water, right where Lieutenant Sampson
had left her, 99 years and 7 months before. Water visibility
looked fair, Hall said; weather reasonably good.

We packed the Boston whalers, hooked them to the two
pickups, and sped to Southport, eighteen miles away. Even
a routine drive with the Watters brothers is usually an adventure, because of their flat-out driving, if nothing else.
On this trip Robert took particular pains (at seventy miles
per hour) to swerve into another lane and demolish a huge
canebrake rattler as it raced frantically for the ditch.

"Ah hate'em," Robert said. "Only two kinds of snakes
Ah don't like; live ones and dead ones."

Southport is the kind of town generally described in
guidebooks as a sleepy fishing village. A century ago it went
by another name, Smithville. Those days it was the headquarters of General Louis Hebert, immediate chief of the
Rebel defenses of Cape Fear. Most of the Cape Fear pilots
were based there. In earlier, quieter times, it was famed as
a summer spa for the wealthy of North Carolina who kept
elaborate summer villas. Now it boasts neither elegance nor
activity. It *does* boast an excellent marina, and we launched
the whalers amid a fair crowd of weekend boatmen.

Bald Head Point is only six miles from Smithville, but the
trip lies across open Atlantic just beyond the tenuous
boundary of the Cape Fear River's mouth. The sea was
rough for sixteen-foot boats plowing along at twenty knots.
Waves ran to three and four feet. Hall and Robert drove
their respective boats from a half-standing position,
crouched over the wheel amidships, absorbing the jarring
crashes with their flexed knees as the stubby craft slugged

from wave to wave with spine-rattling jolts. I could see Jim, in the bow of Robert's boat, clutching a line for dear life to keep from bouncing out, his face drenched with spray, as Robert grinned crookedly at his misery. In Hall's boat I tried to insulate myself against the jolts by kneeling on bunched-up rubberized canvas lifting bags. Eighteen-pound diving belts bounced up and smashed into my legs as we thrashed through the whitecaps, and I wondered if any boat other than a broad-beamed, fiber-glass whaler could take such punishment.

From the air, as he dropped the marker buoy, Hall had fixed *Ella*'s general range by lining up a distant water tank and a warehouse, both miles away on the Carolina mainland. Steering by this rule of thumb he went directly to the marker, a device he had jury-rigged from a crab pot float and tossed from his Piper only two hours before.

"There it is," Hall shouted, throttling down the whaler to circle and retrieve the tiny black buoy that bobbed in the roiling green and white where the Cape Fear breakers began to form. We dropped the anchors.

Somewhere below lay *Ella*, or what was left of her, pounded for a century by the Atlantic's surge.

We saw her easily. Not thirty feet from Hall's buoy a dull, squarish projection came within a foot or two of the surface as a trough passed over it. From above it showed an evil brown color, fuzzed with marine growth. It was about five feet in diameter and it slanted down out of sight.

"That's one of the boilers," Hall said. "It's the only thing on her that big that would still be intact."

As we hastily prepared to dive, I took a moment to enjoy the scene of wild and desolate beauty that surrounded us. Bald Head was less touched by man than it had been in 1864. The dunes that we could see ashore, some 250 yards away, were wilderness now: no Confederate cannon bristled there, no troops would try to drive us away. Man's only track was the tapered brick cylinder of Bald Head light, an ancient beacon familiar to generations of sailors long before the blockade-runners came to Cape Fear.

The only sign of life was a pelican, as squatly efficient as a Navy PBY, gliding alone just outside the breakers that crashed on the Point.

Hall, Robert, and I dropped over the side, leaving Jim— as yet a nondiver—to keep an eye on the surface. I swam immediately to the huge bulk of *Ella*'s boiler. It was a glorious sight underwater, richly festooned with coral and gorgonia, which swayed with the current. A school of closely grouped spadefish cruised by; the largest sheepshead I had ever seen stared at me motionless from below.

Ella's hulk appeared to be broken athwartships. Much of her had settled into the sand, of course, and the water depth was only about twenty feet. She was a fantastic sight in the murky water. I glided past one of her enormous paddle wheels projecting from the sand like something out of a Daliesque painting. Nearby, a ghostly ladder angled down into the flat sand bottom. Coral and sponges grew everywhere.

We began probing the bottom and found it was alive with flounder, scurrying for cover now as we disturbed them, in such profusion that Hall returned to the boat for his Hawaiian sling. Within fifteen minutes the three of us had speared eighteen flounder, all of them three- or four-pounders.

I swam toward the runner's stern, past the giant slanting bulk of the boiler, and passed a huge clump of tangled cable. A brass cutoff valve—evidently a control in the ship's steam system—stood three feet out of the sand. Steel ribs and assorted deck beams were scattered haphazardly, encrusted with orange and yellow marine life. At a bewildering entanglement of wreckage we stopped and, fanning the sand, uncovered a cache of buttons and pins, the first of

Ella's cargo that we had seen. Funny, I thought, how sometimes the most dramatic wrecks yield the most prosaic finds.

Continuing aft we came to a huge piece of wreckage jutting upward from the sand. But digging around it, we found nothing. Then I began probing deep into the bottom with my fish spear, and everywhere it touched there was something solid. Surely the greater portion of the wreck and its cargo lay buried in the ocean bottom.

I turned and began swimming for the one visible paddle wheel, intent on a better look at this amazingly preserved piece of *Ella*'s machinery. Abruptly I was jerked from my course, and the mouthpiece was wrenched from my lips. Wreckage had hooked my regulator hose. I was trapped on the bottom.

Stretching and twisting, I replaced the mouthpiece and tried to reach behind me and free myself from the snag. But with each movement I seemed to become more tightly impaled. I was hampered, too, by the weights I carried and by my festoons of underwater camera gear. The surge of the current was strong, and shoved me painfully against rough prongs of wreckage that were everywhere.

After several minutes of this I began tapping on my tank with the metal base of my camera. Surely Hall or Robert would hear the signal. But more minutes passed, and neither came into view. Visibility in the gloomy green water was dropping now: I could see only about three feet. Again I tried to free my mouthpiece. The coral-encrusted wreckage cut sharply into my hands.

I resumed tapping, and resigned myself to wait for help rather than ditch my gear. But each breath was growing shorter now, and the tank whistled as I exhaled, indicating that little time remained.

At the most, I suppose, I was hung no longer than six or seven minutes before Hall Watters loomed into view. It had seemed interminable. In an instant he freed me from the snag, and we surfaced to replace our tanks.

"Well, thanks for coming—finally," I cracked. "Where the heck were you?"

Hall laughed, "I wasn't more than twelve feet away from you at any time. I just got so busy rooting around for cargo that I didn't hear you, I suppose. Here's what I found."

He handed me a heavy brass padlock, as good as new except for the iron keyhole flap, which had rusted. Somehow it didn't look quite worth all the anxious moments it had caused me.

Soon we were in the water again, where a pair of ten-inch spadefish attached themselves to my activities and followed closely as my digging in the sand released tiny organisms on which they fed.

We uncovered an L-beam that formed the backbone of an interesting mass of conglomerate that included hundreds of buttons, several lumps of coal, and thousands of brass pins all impacted together. We tore the beam from the sand and surrounding wreckage and brought it to the surface.

Finally, the seas that surged through the wreck wore us down. Bruised and cut after a total dive of two hours and twenty minutes, we left the wreck of *Ella*, hoping to return someday with heavier digging equipment to uncover the cargo we knew still lay aboard her.

Jim, who had stayed on the surface, was in only slightly better shape than we. The constant pitching of the boat he occupied had left him seasick. And his feet itched mightily from the bites of sea lice. He had swum to the point where *Ella*'s boiler came almost to the surface, and stood upright on it, to say that he alone had trod the ancient ship and looked to shore, as did her last occupants a century before.

Even the stinging lice failed to dampen his enthusiasm.

It was not until my second dive on *Ella* that I began to realize the significance of this Confederate disaster. On that particular day, as I discovered hundreds of pork chop bones in the bottom of the ill-fated ship, I became aware, for the first time, of the dependence placed upon the block-ade-runners by the Southern people. The bones, of course, were from *Ella*'s 147 barrels of pork. Through diligent research I learned later that this food was consigned to the starving troops of General Lee defending Richmond. But the cargo never reached them.

As one looks back on this 100-year-old drama, one cannot help but be empathetic to the problems of Lee's tired veterans, on quarter rations, yet waiting, hoping, for *Ella*'s cargo to be delivered. In the eyes of the Confederate soldiers, in the cold and muddy trenches around the outskirts of Richmond, the loss of the blockade runner *Ella* was another lost battle, another disillusionment, that ebbed the strength and ultimately broke the back of the Confederacy.

III

ISLE
OF DEVILS

CHAPTER 7

On the Bottom off Bermuda

The offshore reefs fringing Bermuda's flanks are a murderous assortment that have captured more than their share of sailing ships. Not only do the reefs provide a barrier of protection from the greatest seas the Atlantic can concoct, they serve also to separate the tranquil green water and beauty of this present-day, easygoing, vacation and honeymoon paradise from the vast undersea jungle that exists beyond emerald shoals near the shore. Six to ten miles out, Bermuda's ocean is not nearly as placid as it is in the shallows near land. Here magnificent reefs exist like banks on the edge of a gorge. Towering pinnacles rise incomparably from massive coral outcrops. In the background incredible depths occur almost instantly. Should you dare to descend on the brink of this submerged canyon, you would see submarine coral boulders surrounded by great drifts of brilliant sand. You would see a land where distant coral summits appear as mountains beyond, standing tawny and magnificent, their peaks disappearing in the green haze or becoming lost in inky shadows that often preclude visibility.

The whole undersea world here is different. This water is unbelievably clear. Subsurface visibility often reaches two hundred feet. Penetrating sunlight reveals an array of color that can hypnotize even the most unimaginative soul. Once below, among the great reefs, every direction seems filled with suspense and adventure.

The Bermuda islands lie in latitude 32 degrees 19 minutes North, longitude 64 degrees 49 minutes West. The island chain extends only 22 miles from end to end, but is a beautiful sight in the middle of the Atlantic Ocean. They were named for Juan de Bermudez, a Spanish navigator, who discovered them in 1503. English settlement of the islands resulted from the shipwreck of the *Sea Venture* in 1609. She was the flagship of a fleet sent from England to supply food for the starving colonists in Virginia.

Bermuda was originally referred to as the Isle of Devils, mainly because of her devilish shoals and reefs which lured helpless ships into her grasp. Many vessels foundered on the Bermuda reefs, and untold numbers of sailors were drowned within eyesight of the island. These facts were supplemented by further tales, such as the report of a Spaniard, Diego Ramirez, whose vessel ran aground at Bermuda during a storm in 1603, together with four other galleons, all of which were total losses. Their treasure remains on the bottom today.

Ramirez reported the headlands of Bermuda undermined with caves which were homes for thousands of nocturnal birds. He described the birds as being black and white, web-footed, with a long curved beak. Apparently these were the now extinct *cahow*.

"These birds came out from their caves at night with such an outcry and clamor that one cannot help being afraid," he wrote.

Ramirez went on to say that the birds in some way were associated with the Devils of the Island. "The first night that I anchored in the bay I sent a small boat to an inlet to look for water, but none was found. At dusk, such a shrieking filled the air that fear seized us. Only one variety of bird makes this noise, but amidst the outcries some few clearly called, 'Diselo! Diselo!' (Tell them! Tell them!) A seaman said to me, 'What is this devil trying to tell me? Out with it. Let's hear what it is!' I replied, 'A la! These are the devils of Bermuda which they say are hereabouts. The sign of the cross at them! We are Christians!'

"While we were in this confusion the men of the small boat rushed up, exclaiming in their alarm, 'What devils are these? The boat's rudder is broken!' I ordered another to be made immediately because in the morning the coast has to be searched for water. 'Let Venturilla go ashore with an ax and cut a piece of cedar, for the rudder must be made before we sleep.' This man was a Negro and he carried a lantern. The moment he landed and went into the bush, he began to yell, so that I shouted, 'The devils are carrying off the Negro! Everybody ashore!' The men jumped into the boat. The clamor of the birds increased at the cries of the Negro and the signals he made with the lantern. It was these night birds; so many came to the light, and dashed against the Negro, that with a club he could not defend himself against them, nor the men who went after him, either.

"Finally we solved the mystery and brought more than 500 birds to the vessel which with hot water we dressed, and they were so fat and good that every night the men went hunting. We dried and salted more than a thousand for the voyage, and the men ate them all the time. They were so plentiful that four thousand could be killed at the same spot in a single night." *

Another early report from a shipwrecked Spaniard said, "There were some bones of wrecked ships but no sign of people. Since the shoals are so numerous and extend six leagues out from the island to sea, especially on the north-

* From records in the Archives of the Indies, Seville, Spain, and appearing in the *Bermuda Historical Quarterly*, May 1950, Vol. 7, No. 2.

east, ships are doubtless lost far out, but close by the reef there is great depth of water. The currents there are terrible and all run toward the east."

Easterly currents and wild birds were not the only problems suffered by mariners at Bermuda. Once a ship hit the reefs, local inhabitants took charge. In the early days during the settlement of the island, survival of the fittest was the only code. An account of the loss of the Spanish store ship *La Viga*, together with its tender *El Galgo*, describes typical difficulties in 1639.

". . . At about two o'clock in the morning we found ourselves aground, stranded on reefs surrounded by large sharp rocks. It was plain that we were lost and that the same danger inevitably awaited the whole fleet, for they were on the same course. Two guns were fired at once as a warning and, thank God, they altered course and thus escaped catastrophe. But we remained fast where we had stuck. . . . A strong wind dashed the waves against the fragile timbers of the *Viga* and, hastened by the pounding on the rocks, began to shatter them. . . . Soon in the brightness [of the dawn] we could discern land three leagues away which we recognized as Bermuda, a more than welcome sight. Later we saw about half a league ahead of us another stranded vessel which we recognized as the *Galgo*. . . . It appeared that her entire crew had abandoned their ship. . . . A great many small sailing boats with lateen sails were seen coming from the Island, like herons in flight, twisting and turning as they cut through the restless waves. . . . When they reached the *Galgo* their crews clambered aboard and must have found the loot they were seeking. . . .

". . . That afternoon a small vessel approached us. Through an interpreter we were told that they were English and our friends, that they and the Governor would treat us properly and give us a friendly welcome. . . . Numerous small boats were gathered around her [*El Galgo*] and their crews were busy ripping her to pieces to steal whatever they could—like a flock of voracious vultures circling the sky in search of a cadaver and, finding one, pouncing upon it and tearing it apart. . . . They had set their hearts on finding ways of taking from us the money they had judged we had brought with us from the Indies. . . .

". . . The wreck of a ship is a most happy event for the islanders but it makes them covetous and overgreedy to possess the things which their deprivation has made them desire. When such occasions occur, their rapacity knows no limit, and is indulged even at the cost of the shipwrecked men." *

The stories of the Bermuda reefs are sea stories. And like all good stories each chapter is packed with adventure, for theirs is a story of yesterday, when the Spanish galleons sailed. Every year they watched them pass in revue, with their towering poops and their mass of colored canvas. And each year the reefs snatched one or two.

The reefs have seen also the great clippers go coasting by, with a westerly breeze and their skysails set. And on occasion they would reach out with their gigantic pinnacles and grasp a few, just to keep future sailors on their toes.

They have watched the novice steamer crews replace the salts of sail; and have had the rain squalls, the hurricane winds, and the whole buoyant world within their reach, only to trade them for the dawn of another day.

These same reefs can tell a tale about blockade-runners, too, for they have come to know the elusive vessels rather intimately. And on more than one occasion the reefs—those speechless, hidden, devils—have managed to snatch a few that dared to veer too close. Yes, even sleek blockade-runners sometimes met their grief on a long-established Bermuda reef.

* From the *Bermuda Historical Quarterly*, Spring 1961, Vol. 18, No. 1.

CHAPTER 8

Old Blind Isaac's Song —
The Wreck of the *Mary Celeste*

Before the Southern States seceded, the Bermuda Colony was regarded for all practical purposes as an English military outpost. Its trade was limited; its people were humble and content to strive for a meager existence. There was restricted communication with the outside world. And most Bermudians wanted no contact with outsiders. Yet overnight this British island community was swarming with outsiders. Its geographic position only 674 miles from Wilmington, North Carolina, provided a perfect entrepôt in the midst of the Atlantic.

The summer of 1861 saw St. George's Harbour become a Confederate replenishing and jumping-off point. The town of St. George, located at the eastern end of the island, was founded in 1612, only five years after the first landing at Cape Henry and the establishment of Jamestown. During the Civil War its harbor was the primary Bermuda port for vessels engaged in running the blockade. Secessionists, secret agents, European sailors—all seeking their share of the action, thronged the area. Shinbone Alley was en-

tertainment row and offered everything from rum to romance. The blockade-running trade had begun!

The high wages paid for blockade-running drew every
type. And most of the money went as it came, easily and
quickly, like the liquor it bought from the fast-becoming-
prosperous Bermudian wine merchants.

In *Recollections of a Rebel Reefer*, James M. Morgan
describes St. George's in October 1862: "We ran round
the island and entered the picturesque harbor of St. George.
There were eight or ten other blockade-runners lying in the
harbor. . . . Their business was risky, and the penalty of
being caught was severe; they were a reckless lot, and believed in eating, drinking, and being merry, for fear they
would die on the morrow and might miss something.

"Their orgies reminded me of the stories of the way the
pirates in the West Indies spent their time when in their
secret havens. The men who commanded many of these
blockade-runners had probably never before in their lives
received more than fifty to seventy-five dollars a month
for their services; now they received ten thousand dollars
in gold for a round trip, besides being allowed cargo space
to take into the Confederacy, for their own account, goods
which could be sold at a fabulous price.

"In Bermuda these men seemed to suffer from a chronic
thirst which could only be assuaged by champagne, and
one of their amusements was to sit in the windows with
bags of shillings and throw handfuls of the coins to a crowd
of loafing Negroes in the street, to see them scramble. It is
a singular fact that five years after the war not one of these
men had a dollar to bless himself with."

The impact of the great Southern struggle for independence changed the whole economy and pattern of life in
Bermuda. The island folk completely ignored Queen Victoria's Proclamation of Neutrality issued one month after
the outbreak of the Civil War. This proclamation pro-

hibited "all British subjects from taking part, or participating in anyway whatsoever, either by land or sea, in the existing hostilities between the United States and the Confederate States."

But Bermudian ancestors had taught the people of the island well. Few had lost their forefather's touch for turning a fair profit, or taking advantage of an obvious situation. Shocked out of their humble lives they quickly realized the opportunities in transshipping ammunition and supplies between England and the South.

Spurred on by such Bermudians as John Tory Bourne, who lived at Rose Hill overlooking St. George's Harbour, almost all of those who made their home in the colony enthusiastically sympathized with the South. Many old Bermuda families had kinfolk living in the Confederacy and, to them, colony life closely resembled life in the South. Thus, Bermudians devoted their total energies to helping the Southern cause.

Warehouses at St. George's bulged with blankets, shoes, and commissary stores, lead for bullets, and hundreds of stands of arms, all of which had been shipped from England or the Continent and was awaiting shipment to the Confederate States of America. Sections of docks were piled high with anthracite or semibituminous coal, and cotton. It was not unusual to see as many as twenty steamers at anchor in the harbor.

Having always been a maritime people, the names of Bermuda vessels, *Devonshire, Princess Royal, Penguin, Excelsior, Lady of Lyons, Eliza Barss,* and others, were seen continuously as their ships slipped in and out of Bermuda en route to Confederate ports.

Probably one of the most renowned blockade-running vessels to pass in and out of Bermuda's ports was a fast, handsome ship known as the *Mary Celeste*. This relatively small side-wheel steamer of 207 tons made several trips be-

tween Bermuda and the Confederacy. The exact number
of crossings is not known, as she changed her name from
Bijou in early 1864 and confused not only the Yankees but
also those who might possibly have been engaged in main-
taining sailing records for posterity. In addition to the alias
of *Bijou* she was known as *Marie Celeste, Mary Celestia*,
and several other variations.

The career of the *Mary Celeste* was packed with adventure and was typical of many blockade-runners. One of
the first to command her was Captain M. P. Usina. In a
speech before the Confederate Veterans Association of Savannah on July 4, 1893, Captain Usina recalled: "When I
was promoted to the command of the *Mary Celeste*, I was
fortunate to have associated with me as brave and faithful
a set of officers as ever fell to the lot of any man; and I
needed them, for I was the boy Captain, the youngest man
to command a blockade-runner. My chief engineer was
John Sussard of Charleston, and I have never known a better engineer nor a more conscientious Christian gentleman.
I never knew him to take a drink, and I never heard an oath
issue from his lips. Shrinking from anything like notoriety,
he was a true Confederate and as brave as brave could be.
I think one of the best illustrations of his nerve was an incident that occurred on my first voyage in command. We had
succeeded in getting through the blockade off Wilmington
and shaped a course for Bermuda. Daylight found us in the
Gulf Stream, the weather dirty, raining, and a heavy sea,
with our ship small and heavily loaded. The rain clearing
away, there was disclosed to our view a large brig-rigged
steamer within easy gunshot, with all her canvas set, bearing down upon us. I found out afterwards that she was the
steamship *Fulton*, a very fast ship built for the passenger
trade between New York and Havre, France.

"We altered our course head to wind and sea, causing the
chasing steamer to do the same and to take in her sails,

which gave us a little advantage; but she was a large, able ship and made good weather, while our little craft would bury herself clean out of sight, taking the green seas in over the forecastle. Calling Mr. Sussard, I said, 'John, this will never do. That ship will sink us or catch us unless we do better.' He answered in his quiet manner: 'Captain, I am doing all that a sane man dare do!' 'Then,' said I, 'You *must* be insane, and that quick, for it is destruction or Fort Lafayette Prison for us, and I would rather go to the former. I am going to lighten her forward, so that she will go into the sea easier, and you *must* get more revolutions out of the engines.' He went below, and I took forty-five bales of cotton from forward, rolled them abaft the paddles, cut them open, so that the enemy could make no use of them, and threw them overboard. The loose cotton floating in our wake caused him to deviate from his course, occasionally, which helped us some. About this time Sussard sent for me to come down to the engine room, where he said: 'Captain, I am getting all the revolutions possible out of the engines. I am following steam full stroke; this is a new ship, first voyage; these boilers are, I hope, good English iron. All there is now between us and eternity are these boilers. How much steam there is on them I don't know!' He had a kedge anchor made fast to the safety valve. In my opinion it takes a mighty brave man to do that. I went on deck, threw the log and found the ship to be making seventeen miles an hour, into a heavy head sea. 'All right,' I said, 'Keep that up a little while, and there is no ship in the United States Navy that can catch her!' We were soon out of range of the enemy's guns and enabled to reduce the pressure on the boilers."

The summer of 1864 was a busy one for the *Mary Celeste*. It was a trying one, too, for most of her crew; the ports they had to visit exchanging cotton for Confederate supplies were diseased with yellow fever.

Untold numbers of men from other blockade runners had fallen to the dreaded "yellow jack." Bermuda, Nassau, and Wilmington, all raged with sickness and death. On one steamer alone, twenty-eight of a crew of thirty-two were in their bunks. Seven of them were dead. In Nassau, Tom Taylor aboard the *Banshee* counted "seventeen funerals pass before breakfast."

In *Sketches from My Life*, Hobart-Hampden recalled, "When we had only the American Government cruisers to fear, we enjoyed the excitement in the same way as a man enjoys fox-hunting (only, by the way, we were the fox instead of the huntsmen), but when dire disease, in the worst form that yellow jack could take, stalked in amongst us, and reduced our numbers almost hourly, things became too serious to be pleasant.

"However, before the fever showed itself we made one successful round trip . . . we landed 1140 bales of cotton at Bermuda, and it was after we had started from Wilmington on our second trip that the horrid yellow fever broke out among us.

"I believe that every precaution was taken by the government of the island to prevent the disease from spreading, but increased by the drunkenness, dissipation, and dirty habits of the crews of blockade runners, and the wretchedly bad drainage of the town of St. George, it had lately broken out with great violence, and had spread like wildfire, both on the shore and among the shipping. It must have been brought on board our ship by some of the men, who had been spending much time on shore; we had not been twenty-four hours at sea before the fever had got deadly hold on our crew.

"We went to Halifax, where we landed our sick and inhaled some purer air; but it was of no avail. The fever was in the vessel and we could not shake it off. . . . That morning about seven o'clock a man came up from the engine room and while trying to say something to me fell down in a fit, and was dead in half an hour. There was quite a panic among us all, and as if to make things worse to the superstitious sailors, whenever we stopped, several horrid sharks immediately showed themselves swimming round the vessel. The men lost all heart, and would I think have been thankful to have been captured, as a means of escape from what they believed to be a doomed vessel."

In July 1864, *Mary Celeste* left Nassau and shaped her course toward Wilmington. She had taken aboard a valuable cargo of arms and munitions of war consigned to the Confederate States of America for delivery to Richmond.

She had not been long at sea when her Cape Fear pilot, J. W. Anderson, was stricken with yellow fever. The captain of the blockade-runner proposed to return to Nassau, but pilot Anderson demanded that they not turn back. "He would rest when they reached home," he told the captain.

On the second day at sea, pilot Anderson was delirious. Since he was the only Cape Fear pilot on board, considerable anxiety prevailed among the officers and crew with regard to the safety of the ship. How would they bypass the Yankee blockading fleet and make good their entrance among the hidden shoals of New Inlet?

As they approached the Rebel shore in the uncertain light of dawn, a shot rang out from a Union gunboat. The critical hour had arrived: *Mary Celeste* had been spotted by the enemy. Now she must make all possible speed toward the inlet, which was barely visible several miles ahead. Again the blockader fired in hot pursuit. Shells passed through the rigging and burst in the air overhead. Occasionally they would fall short of their mark and plunge into the sea, sending great columns of spray and foam toward the sky.

With pilot Anderson dying in his berth, the officers of the *Mary Celeste* began to realize the impossible situation they had hoped would not befall them. Everyone knew that it was almost certain disaster to attempt to cross New Inlet Bar without a knowledge of the shoals. They knew, too, that the blockade-runner was now in the midst of the Union fleet, for they could see armed vessels closing in from every direction. Capture was imminent if they dared to consider a retreat to seaward.

Lying in his bunk, Anderson had heard the firing and fully realized the predicament of the loyal little runner to which he was assigned. With his head spinning and dizzy in the presence of death, he tried to raise himself from his bed. But he could not.

Noted Carolina historian, James Sprunt, recalled from memory the fate of his old friend on that terrible day in 1864:

"He was too weak to go up, but he demanded to be taken on deck and carried to the man at the wheel. Two strong sailors lifted him and carried him up to the wheelhouse. They stood him on his feet and supported him on either side. His face was as yellow as gold, and his eyes shone like stars. He fixed an unearthly gaze upon the long line of breakers ahead, then upon the dim line of pines that stood higher than the surrounding forest, then at the compass for a moment, and said calmly, 'Hard starboard.' Quickly revolved the wheel under the hands of the helmsman; slowly veered the stern of the rushing steamer, and a shell hurtled over the pilothouse and went surging toward the beach.

"Anderson kept his gaze fixed on the breakers, and in the same calm tone said, 'Steady!' On ploughed the steamer straight for her goal, while the group of men in the pilothouse stood in profound silence but fairly quivering with suppressed excitement. The blockader, finally seeing that it was impossible to overtake her and not desiring to come within range of the big guns of Fort Fisher, abandoned the chase with a farewell shot, and the *Mary Celeste*, now nearly on the bar, slackened her pace a little, and nothing but the swash of the sea and the trembling thud of the ship under the force of the engine could be heard. The dying pilot, though failing fast, continued in the same calm tone to give his directions. They were now crossing the bar, but had passed the most dangerous point, when he bent his head as if to cough, and the horrified men saw the last fatal symptom which immediately precedes dissolution—black vomit—and knew that the end was very near. He knew it too, but gave no sign of fear and continued at his post. His earthly home was now visible to his natural eye—he was almost there where loved ones waited his coming—but nearer still to his spiritual vision was the house not made with hands, eternal in the heavens. At last the bar was safely crossed, smooth water was reached, the engine slowed down, the *Mary Celeste* glided silently into the harbor, stopped her headway gradually, lay still, loosed her anchor chains, dropped her anchor, and as the last loud rattle of her cable ceased, the soul of John William Anderson took its flight to the undiscovered country."

Following the funeral of pilot Anderson the *Mary Celeste* readied for sea and successfully ran the blockade for Bermuda. But because of extensive yellow fever aboard the ship as well as on the island, itself, she was placed under quarantine for more than a month at Bermuda.

After having taken on a cargo of 125 boxes of bacon and 534 cartons classified "merchandise," which included a large quantity of rifles and ammunition, *Mary Celeste* cleared Hamilton Harbour September 6, 1864, under the command of Captain Sinclair. Her Bermuda pilot was an experienced mariner named John Virgin.

The fast little ship made a quick run through the East End channels and was cruising at thirteen knots along the South Shore. About 6:00 P.M. she eased toward land to permit her owner, Colonel Crenshaw, and pilot Virgin to leave the vessel in the vicinity of Gibb's Hill Light House. After a few minutes, First Officer Stuart called the pilot's attention to some breakers ahead, to which it seems Mr. Virgin replied, "I know every rock about here as well as I know my own house." And the pilot refused to take heed to the warning. Seeing the obvious danger, the first mate ordered the helm put hard over. But it was too late. His command had hardly been acknowledged when the *Mary Celeste* struck the reef. She sank in six to eight minutes.

The *Bermuda Royal Gazette* of September 13, 1864, reported the fate of the steamer: "It is our painful duty to record the loss of that beautiful little steamer *Mary Celeste*, so long and favorably known as one of the swiftest and most fortunate of her class. . . . All on board were saved with the exception, we are sorry to say, of the Chief Cook who we are informed, notwithstanding the entreaties of his shipmates to the contrary, went to his state room to save some article which he valued very much, and the door closing tightly after him was there carried down with the vessel. The ship's chronometer was saved by Mr. Henry Adams, one of the crew, who courageously jumped into the sea, and swam to one of the boats then making for the shore, holding the chronometer in the meantime out of the water in one of his hands. The vessel is said to be laid open from her bows to abaft her wheel-house, and hence there seems but little chance of saving the hull. The cargo, however, is being floated out with all possible despatch, and hopes are entertained that the whole of it may be saved, though of course in a somewhat damaged state."

The most significant factor connected with the loss of the *Mary Celeste* was first brought to light by the *Gazette* which said, "It seems to us very mysterious how such an accident should occur in the broad daylight and in smooth water, too. We trust that the Pilot Commissioners will investigate the matter in a rigid, impartial and satisfactory manner and thus throw light upon a subject of the most vital importance. . . ."

The true cause of sinking of the blockade-runner *Mary Celeste* was demanded by Confederate authorities. They charged that Federal spies had paid off pilot John Virgin. Southern sympathizers clamored for reconciliation by the Bermuda government.

The American Consular Records reflect on September 26, 1864, that the U.S. Consul in Bermuda, Charles Maxwell Allen, later tried to clear himself in a statement of his activities:

". . . The only arrival from Wilmington in July was the steamer *Mary Celeste* belonging to Crenshaw Brothers [of Richmond, Virginia]. She lost several men by the epidemic while here. Took in a cargo principally of canned meats and left for Wilmington. Ran into a rock off Bermuda and sank in twenty fathoms in six minutes. Vessel a total loss, cargo nearly so. Much indignation has been manifested toward me on account of the loss of this vessel by Southern parties and I am charged by them of having bought the pilot. I am happy to say there is no evidence to substantiate their charges. . . ."

It was not long before the *Mary Celeste* was forgotten. The Confederacy was in dire need of supplies, and there was little time to pursue a lost issue. "The *Mary Celeste* is gone forever and no one but ol' Davy Jones will ever know how she came to grief," was the way one Bermudian put it.

But he was wrong. Isaac Harvey knew, and for years he would remember. Isaac was a blind man. Although he was unable to *see* the sinking of the *Mary Celeste*, he was there when the survivors came ashore. And he could *hear* better than most normal men. What he heard he put to song, and the tune must have rung a note of truth, for the words were sung and believed from Somerset to St. George's.

Here's how the rumor appeared in the *Bermuda Historical Quarterly*, winter 1954:

OLD BLIND ISAAC'S SONG
"The Wreck of the *Mary Celeste*"

Nearly thirty years ago an old bus driver, Thomas Simmons, who lived near Whale Bay Battery, Somerset, gave this song as a memory of his youth, when it was composed and sung by a blind man, Isaac Harvey, born and bred in Warwick Parish, Bermuda. Simmons remarked at the time: "It's been a long time since the ship was run'd ashore and I have forgotten some of the words." So here we have a little, echoing down the years, of what Old Blind Isaac sang:

> The Mary Celeste was run ashore
> She never will run the Block any more
> So Johnny fill up the glass
> Johnny fill up the glass.
> And we'll all drink stone blind.
>
> How did the Mary Celeste get ashore?
> Oh, Pilot Virgin runned her ashore—
> She'll never run the Block any more
> So Johnny fill up the glass
> And we'll all drink stone blind.
>
> Us boys may just as well go ashore
> We won't be wanted on board any more—
> Now boys we need not mind
> So Johnny fill up the glass
> And we'll all drink stone blind.

Today, Harry Cox, Teddy Tucker, and a few other seafaring Bermudians, can take you to the spot where the *Mary Celeste* sank beneath the waves. If you choose to, you can descend some eighty feet beneath uncertain green water and comb through the remains of this great ship of the past. If you look sharply you'll see the muskets she was carrying to the Confederate States. You will see her rusting and corroded paddle wheels now covered with magnificent growths of beautiful coral and sea fans. And, perhaps, if you search intensely, you might find a bone or two tracing the remains of the Chief Cook.

CHAPTER 9

Confederate Gold Lies Waiting

Ed Walsh was a ship's carpenter from St. George's Bermuda. Like many Bermudians his seafaring blood led him to enjoy a keen taste for adventure. During 1863–1864 his appetite was whetted by monthly wages of almost $200 in gold as a crew member of a blockade-runner. If he were around today, Ed Walsh would tell you that the blockade-running business was a pretty good one.

But he would tell you also that it took courage to run heavily laden cargoes of contraband past numerous warships on duty blockading the entrances of Southern harbors. And it took coolness under fire, as well as fantastic seamanship, to maneuver unarmed runners clear of pursuing steamers with blazing guns.

More often than not the money was well earned. And the bonus, too. Ed Walsh's last ship, *Annie*, almost provided such a bonus. His story—the pieces I was able to put together—is so incredible that at first I hesitated to include it here in association with factual information. But a little research was all that was needed to lure me further. For months it occupied my entire spare time, and now I am convinced that the incredible events presented on the following pages which befell the blockade-runner *Annie* are, as far as anyone shall ever know, almost as they occurred in October 1864.

Annie was a fine, double-propeller steamer with one stack, two masts, and was schooner-rigged. She could attain a speed of thirteen and one-half knots. Her hull was painted the color of the clouds, and her superstructure, what little there was, blended in perfectly. Her stack was small and rakish and her masts could be lowered if need be. Her deck was sharp and efficient-looking and her crew, for the most part, were hand-picked. She carried for fuel the finest Welsh coal, which left no smoke trail. Certainly, *Annie*'s decor and equipment were in keeping with the time. She was a blockade-runner and her crew was proud of it.

During her short life-span she had served her "unknown" owners quite profitably, as well as the Confederate States of America. More than one battle was fought with munitions she had imported. And hundreds of Rebel soldiers would be spared the distress of frostbite in the coming winter months, thanks to the numerous pairs of shoes she recently had stacked upon the docks of Wilmington.

By the end of October 1864, *Annie* had made five successful trips into Southern ports. On each occasion she had been chased furiously by blockading vessels.

On October 31, 1864, she was berthed in Wilmington, taking on an outward-bound cargo consisting of 540 bales of cotton (weighing 700 pounds per bale), 30 tons of pressed tobacco, and 14 casks of spirits of turpentine. Her cargo manifest showed her intended destination to be Nassau, New Providence.

Besides the officers and crew she had just welcomed aboard eleven passengers, among them a Mrs. Johnson and daughter bound for their home in Nassau. In addition, she had recently signed several new hands, all of whom had straggled in from Charleston a few days earlier, having been survivors of the shipwrecked blockade-runner *Constance*, which had been chased and sunk off that port on October 5. Ed Walsh was one of them.

Annie, with Captain Ronnop commanding, cast off her lines early that evening. Soon afterward she eased down-river, waiting for signals from shore before making her dash seaward.

She received the "all clear" sign from the signal station at Nine Mile Battery. Soon the guns of Fort Lamb would be visible. The sky was darkening quickly now, and there appeared an occasional star.

Her crew on deck exchanged hails with several Rebel sentries who could be seen off the port beam silhouetted against a gray sky. They were patrolling the grounds of Fort Buchanan, the back door of Fort Fisher, the South's largest earthwork fortification that guarded the major port of the Confederacy.

A half hour passed before Captain Ronnop received the blinker from the shore battery in the dunes. He had been arguing with the pilot, who was concerned about leaving the safety of the river so early in the evening. But it was the contention of Captain Ronnop that this was the hour at which the tide was highest on the bar, and their chances of running afoul of the shoals would be less likely.

Ed Walsh leaned against the pilothouse, resting a moment, and listened to the debate between Captain Ronnop and the pilot. He had expressed his thoughts earlier in the evening. However, the comments of a ship's carpenter were not especially appreciated. (Just before the last line had been cast off from the quay, Ed Walsh had called the captain's attention to the ill omen of two rats exiting from the ship. Considerable controversy had developed among the superstitious sailors. And Walsh had been reprimanded for inciting the crew.)

But it was dark now, and the tide was right. *Annie* rounded the bend in the narrow channel of the Cape Fear

River and pushed through New Inlet and the open sea. With Zeek's Island abeam to starboard, *Annie*'s bow plowed up brackish water, leaving behind a mud-tinted wake. The crew members were tense. They wanted to get beyond the blockading fleet before they turned to routine duties in preparation for sea. If *Annie* was lucky, they all would be on liberty in Nassau in three days.

New Inlet was difficult enough in daylight. Now, in complete darkness, it tested the skills of the pilot. The shoals were shallow, treacherous, and could snare a ship's bottom.

"All ahead two-thirds," came the order. It was not an unusual command. But tonight it seemed different. Tonight it was strictly business. The tone of the pilot's voice was tense. On the last trip out *Annie* had met with near calamity. She had received continuous fire and stranded on the shoals just off of Fort Fisher. While abandoning ship, half her crew had been captured in a mixed-up affair of uncoordinated panic. The remainder escaped to shore and, with the help of the Confederates, floated her on the high tide, thus saving the vessel. Her original pilot had been taken prisoner by the Yankees, and his replacement was intent on making certain there was no repeat performance of such an unhappy spectacle.

He glanced at the helm and toward the darkened binnacle. They were passing over the bar now. Every step must be a cautious one. Off to port one could barely make out the outline of the unfortunate *Condor*, the speedy British steamer lying on the North Reef near Swash Channel Bar after having been wrecked on her maiden voyage. She held "very valuable stores," including a large quantity of clothing for the Confederate Army. Her three low, raking funnels still could be seen, together with the luxurious pilothouse located amidships.

The pilot glanced in *Condor*'s direction. "What a tragic loss to the South," he thought. "The gold of Rose Greenhow should be lying just off her bow." For a moment, his mind wandered. Only last evening he had shared a mug of rum with the ill-fated skipper of the *Condor*, Captain Hewett. What a shame that such an experienced captain should have to meet with an ill-timed disaster so close to his ultimate destination; and what a pity about Rebel Rose Greenhow. She was a magnificent woman of the South. Her loss would never be reconciled.

In an instant he was alert again, his eyes straining as he stared into the night. "Mind your helm," he said, glancing in the direction of the quartermaster at the wheel.

The churning of *Annie*'s screws sounded ominously loud to the ears of her new pilot. It was such a calm evening that he knew the blockaders would be vigilant. As the smooth runner skirted the shoreline, several blockading men-of-war were plainly visible. One was at anchor, one under way, and another so near that Captain Ronnop swore he could see, through his night glasses, Union sailors on watch on her forecastle. But *Annie* was inside of them all and completely invisible against the background of the distant dunes. She recently had been freshly painted a whitish-blue shade. As she slipped within easy range of the blockader, the pilot wondered whether her presence had been detected. Certainly, veiled by the mist of evening, the vessel should appear to be no more than a mere haze on the horizon.

For a moment the only sound was *Annie*'s propellers, turning cautiously as she slipped through the water, with the sea rushing past her iron hull. Then, in the void of darkness, a shot rang out. A Federal picket boat loaded with marines appeared dead ahead.

Annie's pilot ordered the helm "hard-a-port" in an effort to run down the barge. But the Yankee craft sidestepped the runner and fired a signal rocket with its bow gun to alert the nearby warships. Musketry fire popped in the night as *Annie*'s pilot called for "a full head of steam!"

Nearby, aboard the U.S.S. *Niphon*, officers yelled wildly, spurring their men to action. Bursts of fire and flame flew from the cannon of *Niphon*'s battery as she immediately began pursuit.

Now *Annie* was zigzagging through the Yankee dragnet. Her engines vibrated fiercely and her screws ripped up the water. She tried turning, to reverse her course, and almost ran into the U.S.S. *Wilderness*, which was approaching at full speed. Dead ahead, shells were shrieking and bursting. Behind her, rifles were rattling.

As *Annie* changed course again she was clearly exposed to a thunderous round of fire from the hotly pursuing *Wilderness*. Shot and shell exploded in her midst. Wrapped in a flame of fire and a pall of smoke, *Annie* shuddered and groaned. Her crew held on for dear life.

Aboard the *Wilderness*, officers shouted to their gunnery crews. "See that every shot is true. The old man wants this damned Rebel!"

Another terrible torrent of shot came whizzing over, which was followed by another. *Annie* was literally engulfed in a flame of fire and smoke. Still she continued.

Captain Ronnop shouted at his chief engineer, "Make more steam, blast you! We're hardly doing twelve knots!" Looking back, he saw the two large vessels closing in for the kill.

He turned to size up his position. The shore was no longer visible. But he ascertained he was three miles out, and south-southeast of the inlet. If only he could outdistance them!

"Lord, look at that," he murmured, as he noticed Mrs. Johnson on the deck forward, erect and undismayed, watching the entire affair as if she were at the circus. "She's either the bravest of her sex I've seen, or a most curious old bitch," he thought.

As the resolute runner maintained her course her pilot stepped forward to confer with the captain. "I've a few rockets imported from New York in the cabin," he suggested. "We might throw them Yankees off our trail yet. If we could lose jus' one of them," he continued, "we'd make th' open sea safely."

Captain Ronnop concurred. The pilot sent below for the rockets, hoping to confuse the determined followers. Before his idea could be tested it was too late. Both Union ships fired in unanimous defiance. A shell burst into a cotton bale on the port side, and it became a mass of flame.

Another shell hit the funnel, knocking it to pieces and sending half a dozen men sprawling across the deck, gasping for breath. Splintering fragments fell all around. Several crew members were wounded. Grape shot followed, striking like hot hail.

It was all over. Without a funnel there could be no draft. And without fire there could be no steam. As if she were an apparition in the night, the *Wilderness* overtook the small, fleeing vessel. Captain Ronnop ordered the engines stopped and surrendered.

Already, the Yankee ship was launching a boat with a prize crew aboard. "Stand by to surrender," hailed her captain in a demanding tone.

"My God," thought Ronnop, "the gold!" He shouted for the ship's carpenter.

"Walsh, where are you? To the bridge on the double!"

Ed Walsh forced himself to obey. From his safe perch behind a cotton bale he emerged to the order. He carried a mass of pine plugs, for it was his duty when under fire to plug up any holes caused by enemy shot.

"Aye, aye, sir," he said, running up to his commander.

As the carpenter approached, Captain Ronnop struggled

with a heavy keg, rolling it from his cabin. Beckoning to Walsh he called, "Lend a hand, man, there's gold aboard!"

There was no time for the skipper to explain. Union boats were practically alongside. He ordered Walsh to kick in the head of the keg, and called the crew to help themselves.

"Men," the captain began, "this is Confederate gold! It was entrusted to me for safe delivery. And as motley a crew as you are, I'd gladly turn the whole bloody works over to you before I'd give a single sovereign to a damned Yankee!"

Walsh kicked at the head of the keg. Several others grasped the side to hold it steady. But it would not budge. With blasphemous effort they wrestled with the unwieldy item.

There was so little time. And the cask was too solid. Its lid could not be broken. Cursing and grumbling they worked on it. But the casing would not budge.

Too soon they heard a command from the port quarter. The first from the boarding party was clambering aboard. "Stand as you are and surrender," came the order.

Among the closely gathered crew of the blockade-runner, Lieutenant Ferris whispered to Walsh, "Over here, mate, I'll help you deep-six it!"

The two rolled the keg toward the opposite rail and, as Captain Ronnop watched, pushed it overboard and into the obscurity of the darkened water below. Both men hesitated as they listened for the splash, then turned to face their fate.

It was a desperate moment and all hands were anxious. The Yankee boarding detail was armed with pistols and sabers. One glance at their faces revealed their prime motive. They were interested mainly in the runner's cargo and the prize money they would later share.

The officer in charge strolled forward. "Who's in command of this steamer?" he bellowed.

"I was, until now," answered Captain Ronnop, with equal sternness.

"What is your destination and cargo?" asked the Union officer.

"Mostly cotton, bound for Nassau," replied the skipper of the blockade-runner.

The Yankee sauntered around the bridge. He glanced inside the pilothouse as if admiring its furnishings. Then he turned to Captain Ronnop.

"Show me your papers!" he demanded.

There followed a long night of interrogation. All officers, crew, and passengers aboard the *Annie* were transferred to the *Niphon* for questioning and identification. Some were released; some were sent to prison.

Annie had received thirteen shots from the *Wilderness* and *Niphon* before she, out of necessity, surrendered. The *Wilderness* had to generate a speed of sixteen knots to catch the runner. And even then it was questionable whether she would have succeeded had the shells not struck true.

Annie was first discovered by the *Niphon* at 7:15 P.M. The report of Acting Master Edmund Kemble, commanding the ship, was submitted as follows: ". . . We gave chase and opened fire upon the steamer, keeping her on our starboard beam; the steamer *Wilderness* chasing astern and gaining swiftly upon her, at the same time we used our battery freely. At 7:40 the *Annie* surrendered; at 7:45 was boarded by the boat from the *Wilderness*, at 7:55 was boarded by boats from this vessel, taking the officers, crew, and passengers on board the *Niphon*."

The report from Henry Arey, acting master in command of the *Wilderness*, which was submitted to Rear Admiral D. D. Porter on November 1, 1864, states: "I have the honor to report the capture of the English steamer *Annie*, while running the blockade from New Inlet, by the U.S. steamers *Wilderness* and *Niphon*, at 7:45 P.M. . . ."

And, as if for the benefit of future scuba divers interested in searching for *Annie*'s gold, Master Arey was good enough to list the bearings at the time the vessels were stopped: "Mound Light bearing N. by W. and Bald Head Light W.S.W. ¼ W., in 4½ fathoms of water . . ."

When the Yankee officers learned about the gold, which all of them had come so close to possessing, they were furious. They cursed, shoved, questioned, threatened, and even considered torturing the Rebel officers in an effort to learn its location. But the Confederates pleaded ignorance. Even Captain Ronnop lied that the keg had been thrown overboard "sometime during the chase, he didn't remember exactly when."

Had the Union sailors only known that the fortune lay alongside the quiet runner within easy reach of grappling hooks, they would have jumped at the opportunity of salvaging the loot and sharing it among themselves. In fact, if they had been permitted, they would have gladly spent the remainder of the war seeking the booty that was almost theirs.

The most important report substantiating the valuable cargo was from Lieutenant-Commander P. G. Watmough, senior officer present. He confirmed that *Annie* "has a valuable cargo of cotton (some 500 bales), a lot of tobacco and turpentine. Her papers were all captured, showing that $50,000 in gold had been shipped in her; also a lot of Confederate bonds. The gold and bonds were thrown overboard after the *Annie* had stopped and in view of Acting Master Arey, commanding the *Wilderness*, who endeavored, by firing a rifle to prevent it—it was in 6 fathoms of water and bearings doubtful. . . . I will take such means as are in my power to recover the gold and mail bag."

An interesting turn of events as a result of *Annie*'s capture reflected the anxiety and greed shown by Union ships and their commanders in squabbling over the captured

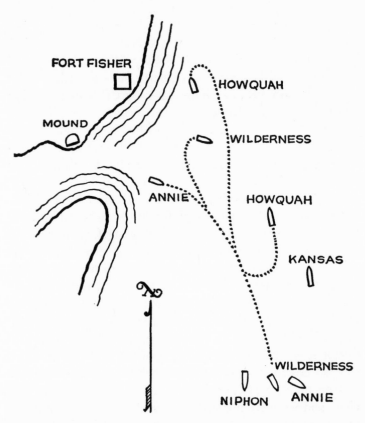

Sketch made from authentic data in the Official Records *shows directions of the chase and positions of Union warships that intercepted and captured the blockade runner Annie. When Annie's keg of gold was thrown overboard in four and a half fathoms, the Mound Light was bearing north by west and the ship was about three miles offshore.*

spoils. Every ship in the neighborhood wanted a share of the prize, and fully expected to get it.

Lieutenant-Commander Watmough reported to Rear Admiral Porter: "The *Wilderness* and *Niphon* both failed to fire rockets in direction of the chase, as directed, but as the vessels were all in sight I was able to get seaward of them and head them off. . . . There was great delay in answering my challenges, and for a time I was suspicious of the character of the vessels. . . . I am satisfied these two officers failed to make the proper, or any, signals indicating the direction of the chase, in order to be able to claim a sole share in her."

In a letter to the judge of the U.S. District Court, Lieutenant-Commander Watmough further emphasized his case: "I have the honor to submit the following facts to support our claim for a share in the prize steamer *Annie* . . . as the *Wilderness* and *Niphon* had both failed to observe the order to fire rockets in direction of the chase, my suspicions were excited by this array, owing to the fact that during the forenoon of the previous day, the *Annie* had been very plain in sight in the river, accompanied by two side-wheel steamers, one having the Rebel flag at her peak, the other an English ensign; the former, together with the *Annie*, had a large number of men in dark clothing exposed to our view, and we were not sure but that they were intended as privateers. We approached these vessels cautiously, keeping across their way, and challenged twice without receiving an answer. The center vessel had a red light up, which was altogether irregular and no recognized signal. Our battery was trained upon them, and orders given to fire the pivot gun to the left of them as a challenge. This was unattended to, except by irregular lights on one of the vessels. . . ."

To settle the bickering, Admiral Porter issued a general order: "While a prize is the reward of the captors, when taken, personal considerations are to be disregarded altogether, and cotton, vessel, and crew are to be sacrificed rather than the least chance should be offered them to escape.

"This war is not being conducted for the benefit of officers or to enrich them by the capture of prizes. . . .

"I feel much dissatisfied at the conduct of the commanders of the *Niphon* and *Wilderness,* and hope while I command this squadron that such conduct may never occur again. Honor and glory should be the watchword of the Navy, and not profit. . . ."

Acting Master Arey of the *Wilderness* pleaded in defense that "It being his first night on the bar duty, having a very short time previously assumed command of the vessel, and that he had not had time to organize; moreover, that the chase was followed so quickly by the capture that he failed to remember the order, or did not think it necessary."

It was not until one hundred years later that, by chance, I came across an obscure and obsolete Bermuda periodical referring to old Ed Walsh and some of his blockade-running adventures. This was my first hint of *Annie's* Confederate gold. And I have spent months since then searching for it on the bottom of the ocean.

Walsh was not sure whether the blockade-runner was stranded and scuttled on the spot or whether she later was removed and converted to Yankee use. But a letter from Acting Volunteer Lieutenant Frank Smith written several days after the blockade-runner's capture confirmed, ". . . The *Annie* was sent with a prize crew to anchor on the day station. . . . Her passengers and crew were sent by *Niphon* to Beaufort."

Of course, if *Annie* was today a wrecked hulk on the ocean's floor it would be a relatively easy matter to locate her remains. And the keg of gold probably would be nestled close alongside the rusting hull. I have been down under the sea on many a wrecked blockade-runner but have yet to find one with a keg of gold lying nearby.

And, I am sure, too, that locating *Annie*'s lost keg will be an extremely difficult task, even for the most persistent treasure diver. The gold could be covered by several feet of shifting sand. The sea bottom in this region can change materially overnight. And, last, but not least—there is a lot of water out there.

But there is something about a treasure that will lure men on. Perhaps, someday, a scuba diver will find it.

IV

DESTINATION: ADVENTURE

⚓

CHAPTER 10

The Steamers That Ran to Charleston

Approaching Charleston, South Carolina, from the sea one first views the point which, since the War of 1812, has been called "The Battery." Here the serene setting of White Point Gardens is embellished with live oak and Spanish moss. Surrounding drives are marked by stylish palmettos. In 1718, within sight of this pleasant park overlooking Charleston Harbor, twenty-two pirates, including the notorious Stede Bonnet, swung by their necks in a single day.

Charlestonians consider it important to live just north of the Battery, but "below Broad Street." This, the oldest section of the city, is considered the "holy land." Most of the old residences in this area were heavily bombarded during the Civil War, and many of the homes that were not completely in shambles have been restored over a period of time.

Architecturally, much of Charleston still retains its eighteenth-century charm. The old "single houses" are built almost upon the sidewalk with their sides facing the street, thus providing privacy for the closed-in yards. Wooden-paneled doors or wrought-iron gateways open majestically through high brick walls leading into picture-book gardens. Walking through fascinating lanes and alleys in the old part of Charleston is like walking through history. In this

scenic sector one can see secluded courts profusely land-
scaped with flowers and shrubs, opening upon spacious
piazzas, their southern exposures designed to catch prevail-
ing breezes.

Charleston is strategically located at the peninsula where
the Ashley and Cooper Rivers flow together about seven
miles from the open sea. During the Civil War the city was
particularly well situated for runs to and from Nassau; and
of equal importance, the harbor entrance offered a variety
of channels to the Yankee-dodging skippers.

The blockade-runners en route to Charleston would depart from Nassau at an appropriate time to permit arrival
off Charleston Harbor at midnight. A usual run would take
about three days. Being long and low, with mast and smoke-
stack lowered, many of these fast little vessels were successful in eluding the Yankee fleet time and again.

A correspondent of the Buffalo *Commercial Advertiser*
in Nassau wrote home, ". . . Every cargo of cotton is worth
from a quarter to a million dollars, and as the *Antonica* has
made six round trips and the *Leopard* the same, they may
well put their fingers to their noses, and laugh about their
packet and their ferry to Charleston. The authorities here
are, of course, not ignorant of all this. The clearances are
taken to Halifax or St. John, but they know perfectly well
the real destination. Nearly every white person is in sym-
pathy with the South, and all are more or less engaged in
these blockade ventures, which are a perfect game of
chance, with chances on the side of the risk. . . ."

The steamers that ran to Charleston were originally
painted a pitch black color to blend in with the darkness of
the night. But famed Confederate Captain James Carlin,
master of the blockade runner *Cecile*, and later the *Ella* and
Annie, started a trend toward cream white or lead gray as
the most desirable color. His theory was proved to be real-
istic. It was dusk or dawn and, at times, broad daylight,

when a runner was in greatest danger of being detected. Therefore, he reasoned, the dull white or lead coloring would match that of the haze on the horizon, or the sand dunes close to shore, and offer greater camouflage, with less chance of being sighted by a patrolling man-of-war.

At first, the blockade-runners docked and unloaded war supplies for the Confederate Army and luxury goods for citizens who could afford them at the Cooper River wharves. But constant Yankee shelling later forced the contraband vessels to use the West Point Mill wharves and other offloading depots around Battery Waring at the end of Tradd Street.

On the outward-bound voyage, a knowledgeable skipper would study from Fort Sumter the positions of the warships off the harbor entrance. At night some of the blockaders usually were at anchor, while others cruised on station farther offshore. If the blockade-runner was able to bypass the inside blockade it was likely that the vessel would clear the outer guard, too. If the runner was spotted before anchored Union vessels could make enough steam to begin the chase, rockets would be fired in the direction of the fleeing steamer, hoping to alert sister blockaders patrolling outside. Then all U.S. ships would converge on the unarmed blockade runner in an effort to trap her in the ever tightening noose.

The men that ran the blockade were alternately praised as benefactors of the South and criticized as mercenary profiteers. Both descriptions often were correct. Although the runners were rushing in cargoes of "hardware" for the army's use, they were, at the same time, draining the gold of the Confederate Treasury for luxury goods from Europe.

The Southern captains and owners of blockade-runners were, for the most part, patriotic Confederates, and each successful run made them heroes. As the need for ships and men to run the blockade increased, more and more English-men and "neutrals" joined in the game. It proved to be worthwhile to do so. A letter from Captain James Carlin dated August 25, 1863, states master's pay as follows: ". . . bringing steamer from Nassau to Charleston, $8000, Confederate currency (about $600 in gold); taking steamer out to Nassau, $2000, payable at Nassau; from Nassau to Wilmington, N.C., $10,000, and Wilmington to Bermuda, $2500 . . ."

Captain F. N. Bonneau received $8000 from the Import-ing and Exporting Company of South Carolina for bringing the blockade-runner *Alice* from Nassau to Charleston. For the return trip to Nassau he was paid $2000 in gold.

As the war dragged on and the South's supply lines re-quired more and more attention, too many blockade-run-ners became sympathetic with the South because of the dollars they were making in supplying her needs. And the needs were not controlled rigidly enough by the Confed-erate government. Soldiers at the front line were starving for lack of food, freezing for lack of clothes, and under-going surgery without chloroform, while blockade-runners risked their lives to bring in cargoes of brandy and cham-pagne, coffee and spice, silks and satin, and even ice cubes for mint juleps.

Today, many Charlestonians feel that the real Charleston is seldom understood by the touring visitors. There are none left, they say, who remember the terrible shelling its citizens endured, or the long struggle to recover from its economic ruin. There is no one around today who can offer a firsthand description of the bombs exploding, fires sweeping the city, or yellow fever plaguing the populace. Gone are the days of the weekly auctions of contraband cargo and the duels in the streets between the crews of blockade-runners in port and the soldiers stationed in town.

But Charleston's archives contain vast stores of letters,

reminiscences, and contemporary accounts of the beleaguered city in the eighteen-sixties. Take, for example, the crumbling and barely legible letters of a Confederate mother; or the preserved correspondence of a Rebel signal officer; or the vivid descriptions of a well-versed old gentleman as he records from memory his days of daring and adventure as a crew member of a blockade-runner. If only those voluminous files could talk, what a story they would tell.

March 12, 1861

"The dearth of public amusement here is made up by the excitement of slipping the blockade. In the last month *thirteen vessels* have run out, and three steamers have come in. . . . How these vessels pass over and through Lincoln's hulks and by the fleet is wonderful. In the history of the war the daring of Southern sailors will form a conspicuous part of the picture. . . ." [1]

October 20, 1861

". . . Captain Wagner of Fort Moultrie gave out that he wanted several thousand cartridge bags in twenty-four hours, for the coast. Some ladies sat up all night, and we rose at daylight. Of course the order was completed. You see everywhere ladies knitting stockings for the soldiers." [2]

April 3, 1862

". . . The very Negroes in the streets are talking of hard times. I heard an old man and maumer in King Street the other day discussing it. . . . 'Hard times—yes, they is so hard, that I think they are almost as bad as the day of judgment'. . ." [3]

[1] Gilman, C. H., "Letters of a Confederate Mother; Charleston in the Sixties," in *Atlantic Monthly*, Vol. 137, pp. 503–515, April 1926.
[2] *Ibid.*
[3] Middleton Correspondence, *South Carolina Historical Magazine*, Vol. 63, p. 165, 1962.

March 27, 1863

"Willie is a paroled prisoner and came home on a walk of two hundred miles from Johnston's army. Notwithstanding *the times,* he and Nina went to a surprise party last night and stayed until the small hours. . . ." [4]

August 8, 1863

"I think winter will find us fighting here if the Yanks don't hurry up tho' in the meantime they may destroy the city by their shells. Here's a chance for your house to have a hole made thro' it by a Yankee ball and render it historical. . . ." [5]

March 5, 1864

". . . The house at no. 36 has been struck again. The shell came thro' the roof into the sewing room and . . . did considerably more damage than the first, but *not* breaking the mirrors. The pieces were scattered all around and one sticking in the wall which I especially charged Robert not to take out, but to leave it for Aunt Janey's satisfaction to show after the war." [6]

January 23, 1865

". . . No law down in this part of town now. Assaults every night or so. The other night they robbed a man here just at our door, and another night pulled one courier off his horse, robbed him and then put him on and sent him off. It is horrible." [7]

February 14, 1865

". . . I am afraid Charleston is doomed . . . we are expecting orders to leave tomorrow or even tonight. My

[4] Gilman, *op. cit.*
[5] Augustine T. Smythe letters, South Carolina Historical Society.
[6] *Ibid.*
[7] *Ibid.*

heart is very sad. Dear old Charleston. To leave her now to these wretches after she has so long withstood their assault. Indeed it is a bitter drop to drink." [8]

August 5, 1865

". . . Two girls came in dressed in homespun, with sun bonnets. They fell into great admiration at the straw hats trimmed with red feathers . . . and immediately, selecting two, put them on. On asking the price, Frank told them five dollars a piece.

" 'Wait a bit,' said one, and stooping a little, she raised her dress, turned down her stocking and handed out the amount in greenbacks. . . .

"We had no greenbacks in circulation, the garrison having arrived only two days previous, so the greenbacks told their own story." [9]

Although the grand old section of Charleston was in shambles from the shelling of the "Swamp Angel" and constant use of other Union far-ranging guns, blockade running was a prosperous business for many well-to-do Charleston merchants. Considerable fortunes were said to have been made. George A. Trenholm testified after the war that his firm was worth a million dollars when the war began. No one knows how much he made during the blockade era, but a great portion of his profits were reinvested in Confederate bonds. "He was the greatest merchant Charleston has ever produced. He kept the books of John Fraser & Company when he was sixteen years old, and later rose to its head. He was a splendid man, from top to toe, entirely selfmade, having only a school education." [10]

[8] *Ibid.*
[9] Gilman, *op. cit.*
[10] From *Life and Recollections of Joseph W. Barnwell,* in the Archives of the South Carolina Historical Society.

The auctioning of goods imported by blockade-runners became a big business, too. All too often the merchandise found its way into the hands of profiteers who thrived on the opportunity of taking advantage of a deprived people. Prices soared sky high. Throngs of traders almost fought to get near enough to bid on provisions of all sorts that were not available locally.

J. Thomas Scharf in his *History of the Confederate States Navy* describes a contemporary account of an auction at Charleston during the war.

"On King and East Bay Streets at least four-fifths of the stores are closed, and on Meeting Street the only oasis one sees in the great desert of suspension is at the houses where the piles of goods which so constantly run the blockade are auctioneered off. Here, when an auction is to take place, merchants, professional characters and men of leisure, all eager for the accumulation of dollars, congregate in vast numbers, and the storerooms present a scene of busy life which contrasts strangely with the remaining portions of the city.

"I have, by the dint of extraordinary perseverance, worked my way into one of these densely packed auction rooms, and found the scene presented one of sufficient interest to describe. A burly man, of about 240 pounds avoirdupois, mounts a chair and announces that the sale is about to commence, continuing with the remarks that the conditions are cash, and that no issue of the Hoyer and Ludwig Confederate plate will be taken. The crier, who possesses a strength of lung of which 'Stentor' himself would have been proud, and a rapidity of articulation that has never been surpassed by human tongue, is accompanied by a little, grey-headed man, who wears a woolen cap of richly variegated hues, the crown of which displays the Confederate flag.

"This little man's chief occupation is to exalt the merits

of the goods on sale, throw in occasional witticisms, and catch the 'winks and blinks' of bidders which the crier overlooks. A wink is as good as a nod with the little man, and he bawls it out as lustily as if he were giving an alarm of fire, or crying 'stop thief.' The great majority of the crowd who attend these cargo sales are German Jews, and one is as much surprised at their numbers as at their unpronounceable and strangely sounding cognomens, which, at the knock down of every article, grate harshly upon the ear of a stranger. . . .

". . . The magnitude of these sales is really surprising, and the last one made by R. A. Pringle & Co., I understand, footed up over $2,500,000. The parties for whose benefit they are chiefly made, viz. John Fraser and Co., have already realized $20,000,000. Of the amount $6,000,000 have been invested in Confederate bonds."

Early in 1865 the flourishing trade of hauling contraband cargo from Nassau to Charleston came to a halt. Fort Sumter was evacuated by the Confederates, and Charleston was yielded to the Federals. The city was abandoned because it was thought that, by amassing all available Confederate forces, Sherman's advancing army might be stopped. In view of the long siege the city had endured, the decision to evacuate was received with desperation and grief by the women there. Compared with the many who had "left for the country" at the outbreak of the shelling, they had chosen to remain to the end, and this they intended to do. In a letter directed to the editor of the *Charleston Mercury* they begged that their plea be taken to the commander-in-chief of the army:

". . . We, women of Charleston, not enthusiastic girls, but women whose hair has whitened through the anguish of this awful war, whose husbands, sons, brothers have died for South Carolina and Charleston, entreat to be heard. We would say that we have listened with grief and horror inexpressible to the hints of abandoning to our foes, without a struggle, the city of our love. We urge by all our titles to regard; we implore, as a greatest boon, fight for Charleston! At every point, fight for every inch, and if our men must die, let them die amid the blazing ruins of our homes; their souls rising upwards on the flames which save our city from the pollution of our enemy. . . . Let there be no excuse for deserting the sacred homes of us and our ancestors. . . ."

CHAPTER 11

Little Hattie, the Most Successful of Them All

A number of blockade-running vessels and their captains distinguished themselves during the War Between the States. Records of seamanship and daring were set and broken almost every month. However, recording with accuracy these accomplishments today is practically impossible. Blockade-runners frequently changed their names to confuse the enemy. Not only was it difficult to keep up with the activities of these vessels during the war, but today the task of research into their past is a monumental job. There are some vessels, though, whose successes can be measured.

One of the first blockade-runners to bring fame to the trade was the 578-ton side-wheel steamer *Theodora*. Prior to her christening as *Theodora*, she had been the packet-ship-turned-privateer *Gordon*. Her name later was changed to *Nassau*. Most of *Theodora*'s blockade-running notoriety came when she was owned by John Fraser and Company of Charleston, South Carolina. One of the first to become her master was Captain John Maffitt. Another of her captains was Thomas J. Lockwood. Under the able leadership of these two geniuses of the sea, *Theodora* made some eighteen successful runs before being captured May 28, 1862, while endeavoring to enter the Cape Fear River to Wilmington.

Another blockade-runner that performed magnificently was the *R. E. Lee*, formerly the Glasgow-to-Belfast packet ship *Giraffe*, which was purchased by the Confederate States of America. Under the command of the brilliant John Wilkinson, this 279-foot vessel made no less than twenty-one successful runs in and out of the Confederacy during 1863. Captain Wilkinson stated that she brought in an immense quantity of war materials otherwise unobtainable in the South, and on combined outward trips hauled almost 7000 bales of cotton worth about $2,000,000 in gold. On her twenty-second run Captain Wilkinson relinquished his command, and the hapless vessel was chased and captured by the U.S. blockader *James Adger* and converted for use by the Yankees.

The British steamer *Herald*, also known as the *Antonica*, was captained by the former U.S. Navy officer Louis M. Coxetter. This blockade-runner made approximately two dozen extremely profitable trips into the Confederacy before being wrecked on Frying Pan Shoals off Cape Fear in December of 1863.

One of the most spectacular vessels to grace the Harbor of Charleston during 1864 was the 300-ton double-propeller steamer *Coquette*. This iron ship was known to have made at least fifteen successful trips into Rebel ports, and the war ended without seeing her captured.

Other highly successful blockade-runners were the steamer *Sirius* (also known as the *Alice* and *Orion*), *Margaret and Jessie* (also known as *Douglas*), *Cornubia* (or *Lady Davis*), *Flora* (or *Kate*), *Ella And Annie*, *Venus*, *Syren* (alias *Lady of Lyons*), and *Pet*, to name a few. A number of sailing vessels, especially those operating between ports in the Gulf of Mexico, were equally important to the Confederate cause, and many of them achieved significant records, too.

The last of the blockade-runners to enter Charleston Harbor was the sleek fast steamer *Hattie* (also known as *Little Hattie*), captained by a dashing young South Carolinian, H. S. Lebby. *Hattie* had been one of the most successful runners in the business. She had made more trips into Charleston than any other steamer. Her success at entering Wilmington had been loudly proclaimed, too. In fact, on one October day in 1864 she successfully ran the blockade off Cape Fear in broad daylight.

On that particular occasion the dauntless Captain Lebby flew every flag he had aboard as he raced eight blockading warships for the safety of New Inlet. "Tell the engineer to crowd on the steam," he said. "Have the firemen feed the furnace with Nassau bacon, . . . run up the Fox and Chicken [the private flag of the *Little Hattie*]. Throw out the Stars and Bars, fling to the breeze every inch of bunting we have on board and, if we must die, we will die game."

The exciting sequence of the *Hattie*'s race for life was witnessed by Mary F. Sanders, who later described the scene for the Archives of the Ladies Memorial Association of Wilmington, North Carolina.

"I sprang to my feet, caught up the powerful field glasses . . . stepped out on the roof of the porch facing the ocean and looked. Sure enough it was the *Little Hattie*, and to my horror, I saw a figure on the paddle-box, whom I knew to be Dan [Daniel S. Stevenson, signal officer aboard the *Hattie*] with flag in hand signaling to the Fort. . . .

"Onward dashed the frail little craft with eight United States steamers following close in her wake, pouring a relentless iron hail after her. When she came near the Fort, the thirteen ships stationed off the mouth of Cape Fear joined in the fray, but He who marks the sparrow's fall, covered her with His hand, and not one of the death-bearing messengers touched the little boat.

"The guns of the Fort were manned, shot and shell, grape and cannister, both hot and cold, belched forth from the iron throats of Parrot, Columbiad, Whitworth and Mortar. This was done to prevent the fleet from forming on the bar and intercepting the *Little Hattie*'s entrance.

"For nearly an hour I stood on the roof watching the exciting race, and when the *Little Hattie* came near enough to discern features, I recognized Captain Lebby with his trumpet, Lt. Clancey with his spyglass and Dan, still standing on the paddle-box with his flag, having served its purpose, resting idly in his hand; and, thus, at 10 o'clock that cloudless October morning was accomplished one of the only two successful trips of a blockade-runner, made by daylight."

Numerous Yankee plots were directed at capturing the *Hattie* but none was successful. She continued to slip in and out of Nassau "like a phantom." On many occasions she brought vast quantities of war materials, and "at least three battles were fought with munitions for which the Confederates had waited, and which she landed safely in their hands." *

One dark night in February, 1865, *Hattie* crept stealthily past twenty Union war vessels that were riding at anchor off the outer bar at the entrance to Charleston Harbor. She safely passed the outside blockade, but as the runner neared the inner line, a gunboat two hundred feet away opened fire. Others joined in and rockets filled the air. For a thunderous fifteen minutes the bewildered little vessel weaved in and out among the roaring guns of the fleet.

Untouched, miraculously, *Hattie* pushed through the shoaling water. She passed into the narrow section of the

* *City of Charleston, South Carolina, Yearbook, 1883.*

channel east of Fort Sumter, and there she met with her closest call. Dead ahead of the speeding vessel, Captain Lebby spotted two barges loaded with Union soldiers on picket duty. Her engine room answered to "Full speed ahead," and somehow the runner's swiftness kept her from being stopped and boarded. However, several of her crew were wounded by rifle fire, and three fingers were blown off one hand of the pilot holding the wheel.

Having eluded that obstacle, she next sighted a monitor in her path which fired repeatedly at the blockade-runner as long as she could be seen. But not a shell struck. They were so close Captain Lebby could hear orders being shouted aboard the monitor. Still, the runner did not falter.

Upon reaching port unharmed, *Hattie* discovered her greatest danger. Charleston was under heavy bombardment. At last it appeared that the end of the long struggle was near. Captain Lebby realized that the hazard of being caught was much greater sitting alongside the dock than at sea. A cargo was quickly hoisted aboard for the outgoing voyage, and about midnight *Hattie* slipped her moorings under a clear, star-filled sky. Just before she sailed, sentinels at Fort Sumter counted "twenty-six Federal block-aders off the harbor." Yet the haughty little vessel made preparations for sea.

Calling upon every maneuver she knew, *Hattie* managed a repeat performance on her outward-bound trip, zigzag-ging through the entire fleet of blockaders. Not once was she sighted, nor did she cause one gun to be fired. At the end of the war *Little Hattie* was found tied up peacefully in Nassau without a care in the world.

Before *Hattie* made fast her lines in Nassau, she and other similar vessels imported an unbelievable quantity of goods for both military and civilian use. Her story is a typical ac-count of many of the blockade-runners that were manned and commanded principally by patriotic Confederates.

While other runners were not nearly as successful as the *Hattie*, they did accomplish notable achievements in view of overwhelming odds. Even after other Southern ports had been closed and the Northern Navy was able to concentrate a greater number of ships off the entrance to Charleston, blockade-runners continued to filter through the Yankee squadron. But the efforts of the blockade-runners were not enough. The grip of the U.S. Navy grew tighter. Finally it strangled the Confederacy.

CHAPTER 12

Legend of Drunken Dick

When hazards at sea are only waves, wind, and hidden reefs they are just as likely to strike at one ship as another. However, when the threats of men in rivalry and war are included, and highly valuable cargoes are placed aboard a ship, the hazards of attack from both man and nature become more heavily concentrated in one direction.

The sea is not always responsible for the adventures that occur upon her. But certainly she is an element that commands the respect of all who come within her reach, for within her grasp lies an immense power—a force capable of turning victory into defeat and success into failure, of allowing life instead of death and escape instead of capture.

With the noose of the Yankee blockade tightening, the fate of a certain number of blockade-runners became inevitable. Some succumbed to the perils of the deep, some were run ashore and wrecked to avoid capture. And some became prizes to the Federal fleet.

The *Beatrice* was a small, 200-ton, side-wheel blockade-runner that was as "fast as a bolt." Previously she had made a successful run to Wilmington, as well as one to Charleston. Her crew was enthusiastic over the swiftness with which they streaked past Yankee blockaders. They were confident, cocky, and determined.

The night was November 27, 1864. *Beatrice* was en route from Nassau when she made land to the southward of Charleston. Never before had she carried such a valuable cargo. Bringing her head around to the north she soon sighted the lightship at Charleston Bar and steered for it at twelve knots. Passing on the outside of the lightship, *Beatrice* slowed her speed and steered directly for Long Island.

She was proceeding in eight feet of water (the vessel drawing six feet eight inches) when her skipper rushed from his quarters on the bridge upon hearing his officer of the deck yell, "Hard a-starboard!"

A large steamer lay directly in front of them.

Beatrice turned on her heels. Aboard the gunboat orders were given to "Pass the shell." A terrific blast resounded.

The captain of the *Beatrice* ordered an intrepid quartermaster known as "Old Cinch" to the wheel. The steady old helmsman took to his job willingly as the chase began. He had once escaped from a similar situation by running down a gunboat, "cutting her half into." On that particular occasion it was said that, "Old Cinch never flinched."

Shells from the pursuer fell wide of their target as *Beatrice* passed into the darkness. Running at her "utmost speed" she was befriended by Providence; and the crew of the blockade-runner cheered as they watched the lights of the blockader drop gradually behind. Old Cinch was again a hero; and relieved of his duty station on the helm, he wandered below for some coffee.

He had hardly taken one gulp of his rancid black liquid when he was again summoned to the bridge. *Beatrice* was passing into Sullivan's Island Channel and had fallen in with another blockader. The situation appeared critical as there was limited sea room in which to maneuver.

At about a half mile, flame suddenly burst out around the

gunboat's side, and a shot came whistling overhead. Old Cinch took the wheel as the captain gave him the order. "Hold your helm!" The two ships were on a collision course now, hardly a few hundred yards apart. The Yankee's guns were beginning to bear.

The skipper's jaw was set. He glanced at the wheel. "Steady as you go!" Cinch nodded. The Yankee continued to bear down upon them, the distance separating the vessels dropping rapidly. The Unionist approached the bow of the runner, and the runner sped toward the Union ship, undeviating. The men on the *Beatrice* could hear excited orders being shouted aboard the Yankee ship as officers directed their gunners.

One cannot help but wonder about the thoughts that raced through the minds of the men aboard the strange steamer lying in the path of the fast-approaching blockade-runner. Most certainly, it was time for a very definite decision, to say the least.

Suddenly, there was no more room in which to maneuver. The blockade-runner's captain turned to his ready quartermaster and with unmistakable clarity ordered, "Full speed ahead and run her down!" The engine room acknowledged his order. Old Cinch held his helm firmly.

Exactly at that moment the Union captain acted. In a terrifying clamor of confusion and speed the gunboat veered off to starboard. Her broadside burst into thunder and fire. The runner shook from the impact of the blow. A shroud parted with a splintering twang, and seamen fell sprawling upon the deck. Amid a blast of heavy smoke and noise several shells tore a destructive course through *Beatrice*'s stack. Still the runner plowed up the water. Other shots found their mark, "below decks, and abaft the wheelhouse."

Nevertheless her escape was almost good. The tenacious blockade-runner flashed past the warship by a hair.

Moments afterward there was a terrible noise behind her as the warship's big 24-pounder roared into the night. Again the air was filled with shot and shell. But when the din of smoke cleared, the lights of the Union vessel could be seen fading in the distance. *Beatrice* pulled away under full steam and disappeared into blackness.

Again her crew rejoiced. They knew no Yankee ship could stop them.

But they didn't know about Drunken Dick.

Shortly before midnight *Beatrice* was making good headway. The worst was behind her now and she was well in toward shore. The topic of conversation among the relaxed crew was Chitty's Tavern, a favorite liberty hangout. One swarthy hand had spent many a happy hour there and, as he put it, "The hostess was so fat she could answer the front door without leaving the kitchen."

Suddenly, the relaxed situation changed for the worse. The chuckles of the crew were interrupted by a heavy, sickening jolt. Those sailors caught off guard were knocked against the hard deck. *Beatrice* had run afoul of Drunken Dick Shoal.

All efforts at backing down failed. The blockade-runner was fast aground. Her crew had just begun to turn to lightening the load when they found themselves surrounded by a large number of Union barges that appeared suddenly out of the darkness of the night. The barge soldiers opened a continuous fire of musketry and boat howitzers.

As the Yankee boats rushed alongside and boarding parties scrambled over *Beatrice*'s port quarter, her captain, pilot, and four or five officers, including Old Cinch, jumped into a small boat which had been lowered on the opposite side. Unseen by the Northerners they slipped off into the blackness of midnight. Thirty of the crew were taken prisoners.

Before setting the *Beatrice* on fire, Union officers recovered "one chronometer, one octant, one barometer, one artificial horizon, one box of blue lights, one salinometer, one binnacle and two boats." They reported that the block-ade-runner had an "assorted . . . and valuable cargo," but nothing else was salvaged.

After burning fiercely, *Beatrice* was declared a total wreck, and the reputation of Drunken Dick Shoal became a legend.

The *Beatrice* was one of the first to grace the bottom of Drunken Dick. But she was not to be the last. In July 1865, after the South collapsed, Navy divers investigated a number of wrecks—all of them blockade-runners—that had met their fate on Drunken Dick.

Acting Volunteer Lieutenant W. L. Churchill, aboard the U.S. schooner *Hope*, reported on July 15, 1865, "I have recovered everything of value from the wreck of the *Beatrice* and the wreck lying near her—name unknown. I have also examined the wreck of the *Minho* and *Prince Albert*: find them sanded so badly that nothing can be recovered. There is still another wreck on Drunken Dick, said to be outward bound and loaded with cotton. She has been there a long time and her cargo is probably worthless. I have looked at her but am not fully satisfied as to her cargo. Have made a partial examination of the wreck of the *Rattlesnake*, lying near Breach Inlet. She is in the surf, and cannot be worked to any advantage."

Today, barely discernible in Drunken Dick's sand-clouded water, rusting remnants of iron-hulled blockade-runners still can be found off Charleston Harbor.

CHAPTER 13

The Capture of Belle Boyd,
Confederate Spy

Almost everyone has heard of Belle Boyd, and most Southerners know something about the exploits of this lady Rebel. She was known to many as the "Siren of the Shenandoah" or the "Rebel Spy." Time and again she intercepted Union messages and passed them on to Confederate leaders operating in the Valley of Virginia. Today, her deeds are legends. Practically every tour of Virginia towns —Winchester and Front Royal, and even Martinsburg, West Virginia, where she was born—points out with pride "the house where Belle Boyd lived."

Belle loved the South with passion. She dedicated her energies completely toward helping the Confederate cause. Most of her adventures as a lady spy were experienced during her late teens, when she was seventeen to twenty years of age. She was reported to be an intelligent, vivacious, and attractive woman, always well dressed and in the spotlight. Belle was tall and shapely, with gray-blue eyes and light brown hair. It is said her features suggested "joyous recklessness."

Belle got her first taste of the invaders from the North

when a Federal search party began pillaging her home. Having been addressed in "a most offensive manner" by a Yankee soldier, she wrote later in her memoirs entitled *Belle Boyd in Camp and Prison*, "I could stand it no longer. My indignation was aroused beyond control, my blood was literally boiling in my veins. I drew my pistol and shot him. He was carried away mortally wounded, and soon after expired."

Belle was a land blockade-runner and, as an officially designated courier, delivered numerous messages through Union lines to Beauregard, Jackson, and other Confederate leaders. She was particularly fond of Turner Ashby, the beloved Rebel colonel known throughout the valley. On several occasions, she rode all night to deliver messages to him about Yankee troop movements. History hints also of the possibility of personal romance, following the delivery to Ashby of such "important" dispatches. However, the colorful Ashby was killed near Harrisonburg on June 6, 1862.

Belle's boldness in advising Stonewall Jackson of the position of Union troops at Front Royal, without any question, led to the Confederate raid of that Virginia town then occupied by the North.

In his autobiography, *I Rode with Stonewall* (published by the University of North Carolina Press in 1940), Major Harry Douglas recalls his rendezvous with Belle Boyd on a wooded hill just outside Front Royal: "Nearly exhausted, and with her hand pressed against her heart, she said in gasps 'I knew it must be Stonewall, when I heard the first gun. Go back quick and tell him that the Yankee force is very small—one regiment of Maryland infantry, several pieces of artillery and several companies of cavalry. Tell him I know, for I went through the camps and got it out of an officer. Tell him to charge right down and he will catch them all. I must hurry back. Goodbye. My love to all the dear boys—and remember if you meet me in town you haven't seen me today.' "

She kissed her hand to him in a farewell wave, and disappeared over the crest of the hill. Major Douglas immediately delivered his message to General Jackson.

The Confederates took Front Royal that afternoon. So quickly did they charge that they completely routed the Federals, who abandoned some $300,000 of commissary stores in their rush to retreat.

Major Douglas relates his next encounter with the lady spy later that afternoon after the Confederates had moved into the town: "I looked for Belle Boyd and found her standing on the pavement in front of a hotel talking with some Federal officers who had been taken prisoner and some of her acquaintances in our army. Her cheeks were rosy with excitement and recent exercise, and her eyes all aflame. When I rode up to speak to her she received me with much surprised cordiality, and as I stooped from my saddle she pinned a crimson rose to my uniform, bidding me remember that it was blood-red and that it was her 'colors.' I left her to join the general."

Soon afterward, however, Front Royal was retaken by the North. Belle Boyd was arrested as a spy and sent to the Old Capital Prison in Washington, D.C.

Belle actually was captured twice. After confinement of relatively short duration she managed, on each occasion, to be freed through an exchange of prisoners. Undaunted, she returned to Virginia to further the cause.

At the time of her second release, Belle had to promise never to return to any area of the South occupied by Northern troops. It was then that she decided to go to Europe to recuperate and regain her health after her stay in prison. She made known her desire to Confederacy President Jefferson Davis. He immediately agreed to the plan and asked her to convey Confederate dispatches for delivery in England.

Toward the end of March 1864, having received her papers from the Confederate Secretary of State, Belle made her way to Wilmington, North Carolina. From that port she was originally scheduled to sail on the blockade-runner *Coquette*. However, because of the dilapidated condition of the railroad, her train was detained, and she did not arrive in Wilmington until several hours after her ship had sailed.

For a number of frustrating weeks Belle waited vigilantly for the right tide and moon. Finally, several blockade-runners arrived. One of these was the sleek British steamer *Greyhound*, commanded by George H. Bier, to whom Belle refers in her book as "Captain Henry." This particular blockade-running skipper was known to her family. He had been a captain in the U.S. Navy prior to the War Between the States. However, at the beginning of the conflict he resigned to take a Confederate command. In addition, he had served on Stonewall Jackson's staff in the Shenandoah Valley. Along with Belle Boyd, another passenger who stepped aboard the *Greyhound* that day was a gentleman by the name of Pollard, editor of the *Richmond Examiner*.

Not overlooking the possibilities of shipwreck or capture at sea, Belle assumed the alias of "Mrs. Lewis." Should the ship fall into the hands of the Yankees, she knew only too well of the heartache and loneliness of life in a Northern prison.

On the moonless night of May 8, 1864, the *Greyhound* slipped her cables, signaled farewell to the spectators on the docks at Wilmington, and eased her bow quietly down the Cape Fear River. Near the mouth of New Inlet she waited patiently as her master sized up the position of the Union blockading fleet.

The *Greyhound* was a three-masted, propeller steamer of about 400 tons. She was painted a lead-gray color with a red streak along the side of her hull. The British-made vessel was practically new and considered a fast ship.

About ten o'clock that evening, her deck piled high with bales of cotton, the *Greyhound* made her dash seaward. Lookouts were stationed in the masthead to watch for a change in position of any ship in the Yankee dragnet.

"It was a night never to be forgotten," Belle recollects, ". . . a night of almost breathless anxiety."

After crossing the "Bar," the *Greyhound* managed to pass the cordon of Federal blockaders without being spotted, probably more because of her invisibility than her speed. The blockade-runner actually passed so close to one gunboat, at anchor about one-half mile offshore of the inlet, that Belle could see Union sailors stationed as lookouts on the warship's bridge. But the night passed without incident.

Dawn broke over a foggy sea. It was Belle's twentieth birthday.

About noon the haze lifted, and just at that moment the masthead lookout yelled, "Sail Ho!" Passengers and crew rushed aft to see a large Union vessel under full steam and with all sails set, bearing down upon them.

Captain Henry called for more steam. Sails were run up on the blockade-runner, too, in an effort to increase the ship's speed. However, it was not long before the distance slackened between the pursuing Yankee craft and the fleeing fugitive.

Belle watched the fast cruiser gain steadily. As the chase continued into the afternoon, she wrote, "A thin, white curl of smoke rose high in the air as the enemy luffed up and presented her formidable broadside. Almost simultaneously with the hissing sound of the shell, as it buried itself in the sea within a few yards of us, came the smothered report of its explosion underwater."

Now that the Yankee was within shooting range, shot after shot burst overhead or fell just short of its mark.

Captain Henry paced the deck of the *Greyhound*, glancing alternately at the compass and yelling into the engine-room tube for more steam.

With shot and shell from the enemy continuing to fall uncomfortably near, the blockade-running captain made known his intentions.

"If it were not for you, Miss Belle, I would beach the ship and burn her, for fear of the Yankees taking any single item of our cargo."

Belle did not hesitate in her reply. "Do what you must, Captain, and do not think of me, for I am in full agreement that we should not leave anything of value for the terrible Yankees."

By now the Union ship was about a half-mile away. The pursuer was recognized as the U.S.S. *Connecticut*, one of the fast, new ships-of-war built expressly for blockade duty. Seeing that it was too late to set the *Greyhound* afire, Captain Henry declared that it was time to surrender. At his command, the *Greyhound* swung around toward the wind and stopped her engines. Just as the vessel surrendered, a shot came hurtling overhead, passing close between Belle and the captain.

"Good Lord!" cried Captain Henry, "Don't they intend to give us quarter? I have surrendered."

As the cruiser came alongside, a loud voice called for the lowering of the British ensign which the contraband steamer had been flying.

Watching two sailors roll a keg containing thirty thousand in gold over the side of the *Greyhound*, Belle Boyd remembered that she must destroy her dispatches. She rushed below and dumped the papers into the ship's fire. Returning to the main deck, Belle found the first of the boarding party coming over the side of the blockade-runner. Captain Henry recognized an old Union Navy friend, Lieutenant Lewis Kempff. The Yankee officer was accompanied by "a smart-alecky ensign, with his greasy hair parted in the middle and wearing lavender kid gloves."

Official Records relate that the fateful day was May 10, 1864. The British steamer *Greyhound* was boarded at 1:40 P.M. Taking the officers of the *Greyhound* on board the U.S.S. *Connecticut*, Lieutenant Kempff left acting Ensign William M. Swasey in charge of the *Greyhound*.

Looking at the haughty ensign, Belle Boyd wrote later in her book published in 1865, "An officer as unfit for authority as any who has ever trodden the decks of a man-of-war." Catching a glimpse of the Southern lady, Swasey strutted over and ordered, "Sergeant of the Guard! Put a man in front of this door and give him orders to stab this woman if she dares come out."

Belle recalled the comments sarcastically in her memoirs: "This order, so highly becoming an officer and a gentleman, so courteous in its language, and withal so necessary to the safety and preservation of the prize, was given in a menacing voice and in the very words I have used."

To her dismay the Union officers swarmed freely over the ship. They helped themselves to Captain Henry's personal wine supply, looted every available locker, and took great pleasure in walking into Belle's private cabin at their own convenience.

The lady spy stood in silence, disgustedly watching the Yankees make fools of themselves. One young ensign walked up to her and said with boldness, "Do you know that it was I who fired the shot that passed close over your head?"

"Was it?" Belle replied coolly. "Should you like to know what I said of the gunner at the time that shot passed over us? That man, whoever he be, is an arrant coward to fire on a defenseless ship after her surrender."

It was not long before still another Union officer came aboard the *Greyhound*. Belle wrote later, "His dark brown hair hung down on his shoulders; his eyes were large and bright. Those who judge of beauty by regularity of feature only could not have pronounced him strictly handsome . . . but the fascination of his manner was such, his every movement was that of a refined gentleman, that my Southern proclivities, strong as they were, yielded for a moment to the impulses of my heart, and I said to myself, 'Oh, what a good fellow that must be.' "

This officer's name was Hardinge. He turned to his arrogant associate Ensign Swasey, and said, "By order of Captain Almy I have come to relieve you of command of this vessel." In the midst of several curses, Swasey handed over the papers and dropped over the side into the boat waiting to return to the *Connecticut*.

Approaching Belle Boyd, Mr. Hardinge said, "I am now in command of this vessel, and I hope you will consider yourself a passenger, not a prisoner." The *Connecticut* took the *Greyhound* in tow and headed northward for Hampton Roads and Fortress Monroe.

Belle retired to her cabin, hoping the more she stayed out of sight, the less chance her captors would have of recognizing her. She feared prison worse than death, and intended using her total resourcefulness in an effort to avoid recognition and capture.

But Belle was more famous than she realized. The Northern editors had written often of her deeds. They specialized in describing her method of luring Union officers into the woods to get from them the information she needed. As she sat in her suite wondering what to do next, the captain of the U.S.S. *Connecticut* was in his cabin, transcribing in his ship's log the details of overtaking the blockade-runner 109 miles East by South of Cape Fear:

". . . She proved to be the Anglo-rebel steamer *Greyhound*, having run the blockade last night from Wilmington, North Carolina, bound to Bermuda, loaded with cotton, tobacco, and turpentine, and having among her passengers the famous rebel lady Miss Belle Boyd and her servant."

Captain Almy had reason to be pleased with his prize. Not only would he share generously in the proceeds of the *Greyhound*'s cargo, but the notoriety he would gain over his capture of the "Siren of the Shenandoah" would go a long way toward a promotion. Furthermore, the episode was the climax to several very successful days. The *Connecticut* had, just the day before, captured the blockade-runner *Minnie* and taken her cargo of cotton, turpentine, and tobacco. More significantly, the commander reported, "Upon searching the prize we found a quantity of gold aboard."

Certainly, the seizure of the *Greyhound* was icing on the cake. Captain Almy reported his conquest in detail to Rear Admiral S. P. Lee, Commander of the North Atlantic Blockading Squadron.

The *Greyhound* "left Wilmington and ran through the blockade last night bound for Bermuda. She has a very valuable cargo on board comprising 800 bales of cotton, 35 tons of tobacco, and 25 casks of turpentine. She threw overboard 20 bales of cotton in endeavoring to avoid capture.

"The captain represents himself as George Henry but his real name is George H. Bier, whom I formerly knew as a lieutenant in the U.S. Navy, and his name appears in the Confederate Navy Register as a lieutenant in that service.

"I have placed officers and a prize crew on board of the *Greyhound* and ordered her to Hampton Roads to report to you. Acting Ensign Samuel Hardinge, Jr., is in charge of her who will give you further information in detail which you may require. . . ."

Upon arrival in Hampton Roads, however, Ensign Hardinge had very little information of a military nature to report. The past two days at sea had been busy ones. But he made the greatest use of his time by declaring his affection for the Southern lady. Hardly forty-eight hours had passed (including several trips to a secluded section of the after deck) before he asked Belle Boyd to be his wife.

After leaving the Capes of the Chesapeake, the *Greyhound* headed for Boston. Although Belle had agreed secretly to marry the Union officer, fear of imprisonment and the chance of escape were constantly in her mind.

When it became known in Boston Harbor that the notorious *Greyhound* with the famous Rebel spy was at anchor there, the newspapers put the city in a state of gossip. The *Boston Post* mentioned the arrival of the blockade-runner on May 20: "The steamer had on board as passengers the famous Rebel spy, Miss Belle Boyd, and Mr. Pollard of Richmond, author of a southern history of the Rebellion. Miss Boyd came on board the steamer at Wilmington as Mrs. Lewis, and her deportment on shipboard is described by the officers as very ladylike." The Boston paper went on to say, "There is much curiosity to see her, but the Marshall is so choice of his charge that but few are gratified."

During the excitement of the blockade-runner's arrival at that port, Ensign Hardinge was in the forward section of the ship giving orders for anchoring the vessel. Having been introduced to the two Boston pilots who boarded the *Greyhound* to bring her in, Belle Boyd and Mr. Pollard invited them to the cabin below for a glass of wine.

Watching for just such a moment, Captain Henry slipped over the side of his captured blockade-runner and into a small dinghy positioned there. He quickly made his way to shore. By the time Ensign Hardinge joined the group, the Rebel skipper had disappeared.

The entire Boston waterfront was probed as an intensive search developed. However, Captain Henry's escape was made good. As the newspapers clamored for retribution, blaming the entire scheme on the cunning Miss Boyd, Captain Henry was crossing the border into Canada.

In the meantime, Ensign Hardinge had left for Washington to try to secure a release for his fiancée. Upon arrival in the capital, however, he received instead the following communication: "For the neglect of duty, in permitting the captain of the prize steamer *Greyhound* under your charge to escape, you are hereby dismissed from the Navy in the United States as an active ensign on temporary service."

Belle, through her own contacts in Washington, and pleading ill health, was permitted to make her way to Canada under the supervision of a Federal marshal. Shortly afterward, she sailed for Liverpool. Rendezvousing there with Hardinge, the couple was married on August 25, 1864. The British *Morning Post* recorded the affair, mentioning that quite a few of English society came to see "the lady whose heroism has made her name so famous and to witness the result of her last captivity, the making captive of the Federal officer under whose guard she was again being conveyed to prison."

CHAPTER 14

⚓

"Them Yankees Made Me Fergit"

It all began at the Virginia Beach dive shop which I operated. One evening I had driven from Richmond to take inventory prior to purchasing equipment for the coming season. It was a cold, squally, wintry night. The hour was late, and for all practical purposes the shop was closed. A thirty-knot wind was howling around the corners of the building which backed up to the ocean front. I was just about ready to call it a day.

Going through several cluttered drawers my eyes focused on an old newspaper clipping which probably had been placed there by one of my divers several years earlier. It was a reprint from the *Wilmington Morning Star*:

"December 16, 1863—Loss of the steamship *Beauregard* . . . During the severe blows Saturday night and last night we learn that the steamship *Beauregard* stranded some distance above Fort Fisher, and has been made a complete wreck. . . ."

Another notation attached to the clipping reflected a quote from *The Richmond Whig* of the same date:

"The steamer *Beauregard* was chased ashore by the blockaders on the night of the 12th . . . some distance above Fort Fisher, near Battery Gatling, and has been set on fire."

I examined the articles more closely. The stain of a coffee mug could be seen imprinted on the paper, too. Evidently, the wreck of the *Beauregard* had been the topic of an evening's conversation some time ago. I chuckled to myself. Same old story, I thought. When the boss is away the divers will play. This was the very purpose of my presence that evening. I wanted to make certain the inventory control was correct. And the only way to be sure was to take the count myself.

At that moment the door of the dive shop was thrown open and with a rush of cold air in walked a stocky fellow and a girl with long, black, wind-blown hair.

I turned around instantly as the entrance of the two startled me. "Hello there," I said.

"Nice shop you have here," said the stranger, walking toward the gas heater and rubbing his hands to warm them. "Is it yours?"

"Yes," I answered. "But business is a little slow this time of the year."

I watched the girl crouch down, her back against the warmth of the flames. Her sharply defined features struck me as would those of a wild and reckless sea nymph. If ever there was a perfect model for a mermaid, she was one.

The man, sensing my eyes were on the female, strolled forward and began conversing.

"Do much diving?" he questioned.

"Quite a bit," I answered. "But it's difficult to accomplish anything in this kind of weather."

"Where do you dive around here?" he asked.

I pointed to the navigational chart on the wall. Its surface was covered with map-tacks and pins bearing the names of nearby shipwrecks.

"There are numerous wrecks within a hundred-mile radius," I began. "The markers with red dots represent World War II vessels that were torpedoed by German subs. There are almost a hundred of them on the bottom nearby. The others, those with the little flags showing the names of the ships, are much older. Many of them represent sailing vessels, mostly with commercial cargoes, or Civil War blockade-runners, loaded with arms and supplies for the Confederate States."

The inquirer listened intently. He had a certain look on his face, as if he were testing my knowledge. In fact, I was certain that was his purpose.

"How do you know about all these shipwrecks?" he asked.

"That's part of the game," said I. "My associates and I have discovered many of them ourselves. The great majority of ships that foundered off this coast are resting in shallow depths of seventy-five feet or less. Most of these vessels sank within sight of land when high winds and thick weather forced them into ever-present shoals. Although these shoals are constantly changing, in some areas they extend seaward more than twenty-five miles. As tides and currents flow, sunken ships are covered and uncovered, just as sand dunes are built up or demolished by the wind and the sea."

The stranger's expression had changed somewhat by now. I watched him as he studied the chart. He was probably in his mid-forties, and his face was etched with wear from outside work. Creases around his eyes possibly indicated many hours at sea. He gave the appearance of being in good physical condition, and I suspected that he knew more about diving than he had yet indicated.

"What about the cargoes of these lost ships?" he asked.

"It depends on the vessel," I replied. "The early coastal trade carried general cargo ranging from railroad ties to lumber, grain, coal, and fish. Ships that went down during times of war usually were carrying munitions and war materials. You can see a buoy flashing out there tonight that marks the wreck of the *Tiger*. She was torpedoed in 1943 with a cargo including jeeps and army trucks. Farther down the coast many a barnacle-encrusted musket has been recovered from rotting timbers of schooners and iron-hulled steamers sunk while running the blockade during 1861–1865."

"Ever salvage anything of value?" he inquired.

I escorted him to the display counter which was crammed full of relics and artifacts from the bottom of the sea. "This is our museum of sunken treasure," I said. Pointing at the case I began describing some of the finds. He seemed especially interested in the items recovered from blockade-runners.

About that time I happened to place on the counter top the old news clipping which I had been holding ever since the couple first entered. It was quite a natural thing to do, and I continued with my documentation of the artifacts. Moments later I noticed that I had lost his interest. He was reading closely the brief account of the old news article I had put down.

A few moments passed. Then he looked up. "The *Beauregard*," he said, in a tone of anxiety. "What do you know of this ship?"

"Absolutely nothing," I responded. "Except that she ran aground in 1863 off what is now Carolina Beach."

"Have you ever seen her?" the stranger asked.

"No," said I. "But I understand she used to be visible some years ago at extreme low water."

"Right," answered the man, loosening up somewhat. "As a boy I used to climb upon her machinery at low tide. But that was before the inlet was cut through near Carolina Beach. Later, hurricane Hazel pretty well flattened her out. She's farther offshore now and seldom visible anymore."

"Then you know the ship," I remarked.

Before he could answer, the girl left her perch by the

heater and joined us. Casting a provocative glance in my direction she leaned on the counter.

"Go ahead and tell him," she said to her boyfriend with the leathery face. "The diver here looks like a live one, and he might like a piece of the action!"

Her male companion didn't appreciate the glance she gave me, but apparently he was used to such distractions. I soon coaxed him to tell his tale. At first I figured it would be just another sea story.

After a brief introduction, he related the following account, which I've never to this day been able to prove or disprove. But his name must not be mentioned for reasons that soon will become obvious. So real and down-to-earth did his words ring that I remember them almost exactly as he told them that night. As he began, the wind whistled and moaned around the eaves and through the shutters. He pulled up a stool and the vixen next to him relaxed in an extremely casual slouch against the counter. From the corner of my eye I could see her giving me the once over. Apparently they were not conscious of the late hour.

"Yes, I know something about the blockade-runners," he began. "I've salvaged Whitworth and Parrott shells from the *Ella* off Bald Head Point, and brought up probably a ton of copper and brass from the return lines, valves and flanges around her boiler.

"I worked for ten years as a hard-hat diver out of Morehead City, cutting up some of those merchant wrecks beyond the ten-fathom line. And believe me, those Morehead shipwrecks are home for some of the biggest sharks you'll see.

"But as to the blockade-runner *Beauregard*, I reckon I know more about that ship than any man alive. Her real name was *General Beauregard*, after the famous Confederate leader. She also used the alias *Havelock*. She was owned by the Chicora Company, one of the more successful blockade-running businesses out of Charleston, South Carolina.

"She was a steamer of 824 tons and carried a crew of forty-seven. The *Official Records of the Union and Confederate Navies* report the *Beauregard* as having been chased ashore by the U.S.S. *Howquah*. The *Records* state her location to be between what used to be known as Flag Pond Hill and Dick's Bay.

"At the time *Beauregard* struck the beach she was outward bound. Previously the ship had made thirteen successful runs between Wilmington and Bermuda, and Charleston to Nassau; an extremely prosperous career as blockade-runners were judged, to say the least.

"But the most fascinating account of her last trip was the fact that she had aboard, together with her load of cotton and turpentine, a shipment of gold."

At the mention of that magical word, *gold,* I tried to interrupt the storyteller, but it was his tale and he fully intended to continue. By then torrents of rain were striking the windows. The roar of the surf pounding upon the beach coupled with the howling of the wind created an eerie atmosphere in the small shop. Taking time only to cast a glance outside to check the progress of the weather he began again.

"My grandpa was the one that started it all," he said. "His father actually sailed aboard the *Beauregard* and was at the helm when she was wrecked. The story has been passed down through the family in one version or another for years and years. But about one thing I am certain, there was gold aboard that vessel when she sank, and there's gold aboard her today. My grandpa never lied.

"You see, the *Beauregard* was outward bound for Bermuda. The gold was on consignment to a British export house in payment for previously contracted supplies. The English jobbers were beginning to doubt the value of Confederate Notes, so they began insisting on payment in gold.

"About eight in the evening on the night she sank, things began looking bad for the blockade-runner when the U.S.S. *Howquah* spotted her running parallel with the beach. The Yankee cruiser put on full steam and gradually forced the runner closer and closer to shore. The way the coastline bends around to the north the Federals knew they'd cut her off sooner or later. What's more, a northeasterly was blowing, and with the heavy cargo of cotton, the *Beauregard*'s speed was curtailed considerably.

"When the *Beauregard*'s captain realized what was happening he had to act fast. The only possible alternative was to run the ship as close upon the beach as possible in an effort to save the cargo. This is exactly what he did.

"But the villain in the plot was the terrible weather as much as the speed and gunfire of the Yankee warship. The runner being of extremely shallow draft, and very long and low, provided little resistance to the oncoming breakers from out of the northeast. When the ship struck, the seas rolled over her unmercifully. It was all the crew could do to lower the boats and save themselves, much less the cargo. One of the boats capsized almost immediately. The other made it to shore, but the port side was almost completely stove in. As far as I know, all of the crew could swim, and most of the men jumped free and let the breakers carry them in. They would have frozen to death if a band of Confederates hadn't appeared, who built a fire behind the dunes to warm the water-soaked mariners.

"Of course, the crew planned to return the next morning when the seas subsided. They thought they could save the gold as well as salvage a good portion of the cotton. But they were mistaken.

"The northeaster lasted for three days. And during daylight hours practically the entire Union fleet held target practice on the stranded *Beauregard*. The ship was severely damaged from the Yankee fusillade, and the heavy seas beat her to pieces. By the third morning, all of the *Beauregard's* decks were submerged. Any attempt at salvage was impracticable.

"The story gets a little hazy at this point. But it was supposed that there was no immediate salvage performed. I guess things were happening so fast there were too many other blockade-runners to worry about. The sinking of the *Antonica* a few days later created an equal disaster, as she was carrying a full load of liquor and clothing. So the *Beauregard* was forgotten.

"Most of *Beauregard's* crew signed aboard other blockade-runners. Grandpa's old man asked for leave to go home to tell everybody about his blockade-running adventures. Having had several close calls, he was in no hurry to return to sea, and he stayed home long enough to help with the spring planting.

"In April 1864 he signed aboard the runner *Greyhound* out of Charleston. But his luck had run out. The ship was captured soon afterwards and he was taken prisoner. Most of his shipmates were British or French sailors who were held for a while, then released. But great-grandpa didn't hesitate to tell a couple of Union officers where they could go when they tried to interrogate him . . . so they locked him up for the duration. He served almost a year in prison, and things must have been pretty tough on him.

"Grandpa used to tell me about the conditions his father suffered through during those times. Apparently, he never was the same again. You wouldn't be either if you had to live for a year with rats and vermin and sick or dying inmates as companions.

"Well, the war finally ended, and the old man came home. His health was poor, and he was never strong enough to do much work. He spent his last days on the front porch in the rocker or wandering around the countryside visiting his old seafaring buddies. We lived near the coast, and he'd spend days on end watching the ships come and go.

"Before he died he told grandpa about his blockade-running days and especially about being shipwrecked on the *Beauregard*. Grandpa was just a youngster then, but he took it all in. However, each time he'd question his father about the wreck of the *Beauregard* and the whereabouts of the gold the old veteran just stared blankly at him and replied something like, 'Ah don't rightly remember, sonny boy, cause in prison things were bad, always bad, and them Yankees made me fergit, but I'll think of it by and by.'

"The truth is that toward the end, the poor old fellow was a little loony. But that didn't bother grandpa. He was particularly fond of him and was the only one in the family that paid him any attention. He'd sit for hours listening to the old hero spin his yarns with a faraway gaze in his eyes.

"When great-grandfather died he willed a map to grandpa. Except for a few battered personal belongings the map constituted his entire estate. It was crudely drawn, and the information it contained was sketchy. But grandpa was certainly proud of that map, for it showed the location of the *Beauregard* and told about the cargo of gold. I have it in my possession today.

"Now, our family always has been of seagoing lineage. In fact, my ancestors were shipwrecked off Portsmouth Island near Ocracoke. Grandpa didn't take to the sea as much as his father, but there must have been some salt in his blood somewhere for he was determined to go after the *Beauregard*'s gold.

"He had been told many times how his father had helped carry the strongbox aboard the blockade-runner and how he had placed it under the captain's bunk on the starboard side of the ship. Although of small construction and with hand-tempered bolts spaced equidistantly, the chest was heavy enough to require two men to carry it aboard. Whether the gold was in bar or coin form he never said, but it was one helluva heavy box. He reckoned there must have been between sixty and seventy-five thousand dollars in treasure in that little chest. It would be worth twice that amount in today's money market.

"Over a period of years, grandpa did a lot of talking and actually made a couple of feeble salvage attempts on the wrecked *Beauregard*. But his efforts amounted to little more than free diving in its crudest form. You can understand the problem, though, as the wreck lies directly in the surf zone, and the surge and backwash are extremely rough. It's practically impossible for a salvage boat to anchor near the hulk, and even though there is little water depth, the bottom is hazardous around the wreck. Of course, grandpa didn't have the benefit of modern diving gear, and the rusting iron hull was deeply sanded in, just as it is today.

"After a few tries at salvage, grandpa looked all over for other divers. But he never found anyone he could trust enough to share the secret. He knew he'd have to cut someone else in on the loot, and he worried and fretted over this for well on to fifty years.

"The fact is, grandpa ended up just like his old man. He spent the last years of his life dreaming about the gold aboard the *Beauregard*. The thought of treasure sometimes does funny things even to an honest man, and grandpa wanted that gold so badly, yet was so unwilling to share the find, that he lost it completely.

"And, that's the purpose of my visit tonight," the stranger said, in summary. "I don't intend to end up like the others who have known about the *Beauregard*. That gold is justifiably mine—either by inheritance or destiny. But I'm willing to split it fifty-fifty with the right man. Now, I've heard a lot about your diving activities in this area. And the folks with whom I checked said you could be trusted. You've got the boat and equipment, and I've got the map and location. What do you say?"

That is exactly how the story began. I had known of the *Beauregard*, but not of her gold. Numerous shipwrecks exist in this region, yet few people know what might be hidden within their sunken hulks.

Initially the tale seemed to have some merit. Great quantities of gold were shipped out of the Confederacy aboard the blockade-runners, and some was lost. Could the stranger's story be true? I wondered. The *Beauregard* was beached extremely close to shore. The wreck was visible for many years. Could the treasure still be there?

This was the question that kept me awake for many nights, and still does. After long hours of research, however, I still did not have the answer. Nowhere could I find authentic reference to the tale. Still I knew, too, that if there really existed recorded directions to a pile of money like this, someone would have long ago picked it out of the water. Sometimes the only clue to lost loot comes from a closely guarded family secret. Many discoveries have come in the past from source material known only to one person.

After research efforts failed, I began to talk to some of the old timers. My contacts extended to bank presidents, barkeepers, commercial fishermen, and local historians.

Finally, one or two old sea dogs in the area remembered. Yes, there had been a rumor through the years about the *Beauregard*. No one could be certain, of course, but they had heard some talk about the gold somewhere along the way. The longer I questioned them the more certain they became.

Whenever an opportunity presented itself, I visited the site of the *Beauregard*. Exploratory dives, or I should say "probes," were hardly productive. Although water depth is extremely shallow, the wreck site consists of little more than a pile of jagged, rusting iron and tons of shifting sand.

Breakers roll incessantly over the wreck, and the undertow is beyond description. Subsurface visibility is at best six inches, and, in fact, on some days one eye might very well view something the other eye does not.

Gradually my meetings with the man with the leathery face and the girl with the long black hair became less frequent. His own enthusiasm continued, and the girl most certainly possessed those undefined qualities that lure men on. But factors that have doomed so many treasure hunts caused this one never to get off the ground.

There was no documentary evidence. The only positive information came verbally and the sources were unknown. The problems of never enough time, continuous bad weather, lack of funds, and other business commitments forced me to forget about the *Beauregard* and her gold; at least, for the present.

It is conceivable that beneath the sands off Carolina Beach a small fortune may be waiting for some lucky finder. On the other hand, the gold may have been removed shortly after the ship was wrecked. Possibly, the treasure never existed in the first place.

To those interested in searching further I offer this conclusive comment. The legend of the *Beauregard* is but a part of the enchantment of this area. There *is* treasure nearby. It exists all along the shell-strewn beaches and in the fish-filled gullies along the shore. It literally abounds in the honking of wild geese in flight overhead or in the radio garble of the sport fishermen as a billfish is boated. And in the museums, churches, and seafood restaurants it is discovered almost every day.

CHAPTER 15

Laughing Sharks and Yankee Cannon

Generally the world beneath the sea is a friendly place, and experienced divers do not always accept as true the many tales of undersea creatures and their vicious habits. But there are hazards associated with this briny environment, just as there are dangers in crossing the street.

One of the most disconcerting of all underwater environmental factors is the unpredictability of the shark. Nobody really knows what a shark is going to do. Although some species of sharks are definitely more aggressive than others, any shark's primary motivation is survival of the fittest. This fact usually determines what the diver's standard rule should be in dealing with one: *Get out of the water*.

Sharks are primarily fish eaters. But their diet can include a great variety of unbelievable and undigestible items ranging from bottles to barrels. It has been proven over the years that man occasionally falls into this dietary category.

Robert Watters concurs with this statement.

"We were swimmin' along and happened to look around and saw a twelve-foot lemon shark so close I could've reached out and touched him. Brother Hall had a five-foot spear and he jabbed at the monster two or three times. This didn't seem to phase the critter, so with our scuba gear we swam inside the ol' shipwreck 'til he was gone.

"We ducked under a couple of big beams lying athwart-ship and waited 'bout five minutes. Then we swam back to our down-line and looked around. Visibility was pretty good and we didn't see the shark so we shot back to the surface.

"Hall had just gotten in the boat when the shark reappeared, heading straight for me. I was so scared that when the big devil rolled over and opened his mouth to invite me to supper I just sort of inhaled myself right out of the water and into the boat. The weight belt slid off my hip and dropped to the bottom just as if I'd throw'd it down there. It's still on the sea floor today, and you can have it if you want to go git it."

That was Robert Watters' first and last visit to the sunken remains of the *Peterhoff*. His brother, Hall, has visited this shipwreck site on several occasions since then. Each time the water was thick with sharks. On one particular trip there were a number of skilled Navy divers present. However, the sharks chose not to challenge them.

The *Peterhoff* was a screw-propeller steamer of 1200 tons. She was 210 feet in length, 28 feet wide, with a hold 15 feet in depth. As a Federal blockader she carried a crew of 124 men and was armed with seven guns.

The tale of the *Peterhoff* belongs to Hall Watters, for it was he who found the sunken ship and first discovered its cannon. Our mutual friend, Charles Foard, of Wilmington, North Carolina, also deserves special mention. Had it not been for Foard's relentless research on blockade-runner history, Hall would not have been motivated to search out the location of this particular wreck. There are hundreds of shipwrecks in the Cape Fear area, many of them blockade-runners. But the story of the *Peterhoff* is in a class all its own. The fact that the greater portion of this historic ship is still well preserved in relatively shallow water should prove to be of continued interest to ambitious scuba divers and historians in the eastern North Carolina territory.

The account of the *Peterhoff* was related to me in a delightful North Carolina accent that made the unique discovery of this lost shipwreck even more appealing. Although North Carolina is considered the Tarheel State, when a Carolinian refers to being *tarred*, it means he's *tired;* when he *lacks* something, he *likes* it; when he's *hair*, it means he's *here;* and when he's *fustrated*, he's *tops*, or initially ranked. Thus it can be stated that Hall Watters is a fustrate friend.

" 'Bout two years ago," Hall began, one Sunday afternoon as we cleaned artifacts recently recovered from a nearby shipwreck, "the North Carolina Department of Archives and History wanted some large guns for the Fort Fisher Historical Center. Ol' Cholly Foard learned of this, and without batting an eye suggested they get 'em from the U.S.S. *Peterhoff.* The local historians knew that the *Peterhoff* was a Yankee blockader that had sunk off the coast, but nobody around these parts had any idea as to its location. Ol' Cholly had a 1866 chart of the Cape Fear area, and one or two of the landmarks appearing on that map were still in existence today. With this information and the data in the logbook of the *Peterhoff* at the time of her sinking, we figgered we could find 'er."

As Hall rambled on about the background of the ship, I reviewed his file of official data that had been accumulated on the history of the *Peterhoff.*

Originally the *Peterhoff* had served as the Emperor of Russia's royal yacht. She had been acquired by Rebel interests and was outfitted as a blockade-runner. The ship left Liverpool in January of 1863 with a cargo of shoes, blankets, clothes, and medicine consigned to the Confederate States of America. However, the Yankees had been alerted as to the nature of her mission, and all U.S. Navy ships of the North Atlantic Blockading Squadron were on the lookout for this suspicious steamer.

In February of 1863 the U.S.S. *Alabama* spotted the *Peterhoff* entering St. Thomas in the Virgin Islands and examined her papers. The commander of the *Alabama* apparently found everything in order and let her go. However, five days later, just as the blockade-runner had cleared the harbor of St. Thomas, she was stopped and boarded by men of the U.S.S. *Vanderbilt*. Lieutenant Baldwin, in command of the *Vanderbilt*, reported that the *Peterhoff*'s papers were *not* in order. She displayed a manifest for seven boxes of tea, but in the boxes were fieldpieces, arms and ammunition. Furthermore, one man was caught throwing a pile of papers and documents overboard. He later admitted being a Confederate agent.

So the blockade-runner, which failed to make a single successful trip, was taken by the Unionists as a prize. A year later the ship had been converted for U.S. Naval service and was assigned to blockade duty off Wilmington.

She had served in this capacity for a week when at five o'clock in the morning of March 6, 1864, a lubberly ensign in command of the deck of the U.S.S. *Monticello* ran right into the *Peterhoff*, striking the vessel amidships. The *Peterhoff* sank in thirty minutes in five and a half fathoms. All officers and crew were saved, but the ship was a total loss.

The U.S. warships *Niphon* and *Mount Vernon* were sent to destroy all articles that might later be salvaged by the Rebels. The masts of the *Peterhoff* were cut away, and all guns that could be reached were spiked and shoved overboard. The gunboat was left and forgotten for just about a hundred years.

"One day while flying for the commercial fishin' fleet," Hall continued, "I noticed some discoloration in the water below, which I knew was too stationary to be a school of fish. I got a range on Bald Head Light that was bearing just about southwest, three quarters west, and it occurred to me that this was the same bearing given by the *Official Records* the day the *Peterhoff* sank back in 1864. I took a fix on Fort Fisher, too. This gave me a good cross-reference.

"Returning to the airport, I rigged up a buoy float and dropped it a little while later to mark the discolored water. This was on a Friday, and since we weren't fishin' the next day, Robert and myself decided to investigate that shadow lying below my buoy.

"Course we didn't realize at the time that there were so many sharks in the area. On our first dive we had hardly entered the water when we saw the big one. Then, later, there were several more. Most of the sharks were just curious. But the one that struck at Robert must've read a different book.

"We were leaving the water when the thing appeared. The shark struck at Robert just as he was entering the boat, and it really shook us up. Since Robert had dropped his weight belt we thought we'd stay in the boat for fifteen minutes and then go back for it. But the shark had other ideas. He wouldn't leave. In fact, he brought some friends. Just when we'd begin to think they had disappeared, one or two of 'em would swim up by the boat. The rascals would actually stick their heads out of the water as if they were laughing at us. Several of them had fang-like teeth that protruded externally above their gums. They'd swim by and grin like fools. But any one of 'em was capable of taking a good hunk out of us. I paunched * one big fella with the spear when he came swimmin' close by the boat, but it didn't even slow him down.

"We were only able to stay down long enough to see that the wreck was a large vessel. She was lying in a south-easterly direction with her stern toward shore in about thirty-five feet of water. The hull was pretty well intact.

* "Paunch"—Carolina blow or jab.

And the wreck was really a beautiful sight. Sheepshead and tautog were swimmin' all around, and the covering of marine growth was amazing."

Watters was almost certain that this was the wreck of the *Peterhoff*. Spurred on by enthusiasm he contacted Lieutenant-Commander J. L. Bull, III, of the Submarine Rescue vessel, U.S.S. *Petrel*, who took special leave to dive with him on the sunken ship. They were able to stay on the wreck long enough to locate three large 32-pounder cannon on the main deck, one still on its carriage. A tremendous hole in the side of the wreck revealed that the *Peterhoff* had been struck amidships, slightly forward of the engine on the starboard side.

"That day the water visibility on the bottom of the ocean was the best I'd ever known it," Hall continued. "As I swam by the engine, several of the cannon were in plain sight, which was quite a distance. They were heavily encrusted with marine growth. The ship was over two hundred feet in length and a good part of her hull was visible. The anchor could be seen; the taffrail was still intact around the stern; and the stack, riddled with holes from shot and shell, had fallen across the deck. We didn't enter the superstructure to any extent. But I'm convinced there's a lot to be found inside her."

Following this dive the explorers became excited over the prospect of raising the cannon. They had hopes of discovering other valuable relics, too. Navy divers, under Bull's direction, were brought to the site. Stanley South, the local archaeologist for the North Carolina Department of Archives and History, coordinated the salvage activities. He was assisted by John Miller of the Processing Laboratory. Governor Terry Sanford and other officials also were enthusiastic about raising the guns, as was Rear Admiral E. M. Eller, Director of Naval History in Washington, D.C.

On July 30, 1963, the cabin cruiser *Coquina* anchored

over the wreck. It took about two hours to raise the first heavy gun to the surface.

"While we were attaching the straps around the cannon and hooking up the inflatable bag, two sharks swam by. So the commander asked me to ride shotgun while the Navy boys finished the work. This time I had a twelve-gauge shell at the end of my spear."

Hall said that it took about 450 cubic feet of air to get the 7200-pound cannon off the bottom. The gun was partially sunk in the sand, and there were several beams and jagged wreckage lying nearby.

"Getting the thing ashore was the problem. We floated the gun under the inflated lifting bag, while the *Coquina* towed the cannon within five hundred feet of the beach. At that point the Navy divers deflated the bag slightly and shifted it under the large gun in order to bring the cannon through the surf. A line was then connected with a bulldozer on the beach which dragged the big gun to shore. Samuel Townsend, Chief Preservationist for the Department of Archives and History, was in charge of the processing and cleaning.

"It took a couple of additional days to raise the other cannon. While the divers were working on that project I did a little exploring on my own. There's at least two smaller brass guns down there. I think they're field artillery pieces weighing around seven hundred pounds. I marked the spot and covered one of the more obvious brass pieces with sand so the other divers wouldn't recognize it. We'll go back and get it one day. The whistle is still on the funnel, too.

"I also picked up some brass straps off the gun port, some brass pins and a few other odds and ends. The Navy boys found a lead commode, and nothing would satisfy them 'til they brought it to the surface. They planned to take it back to the base and install it in the Waves' quarters."

The guns that were recovered, both 32-pounders, were dated 1847. The larger cannon weighed 7200 pounds and was over 10 feet long. The smaller one was 9 feet in length and weighed 6400 pounds. Plans are now being made to display these handsome relics at the Fort Fisher Visitor Center Museum.

The remaining cannon, together with the brass field-pieces, are still resting on the bottom of the ocean. Someday, a scuba diver will get them . . . if a shark "don't git him first."

V

———◆———

NASSAU—EL DORADO
OF ADVENTURERS

CHAPTER 16

High Wages and Low Morals

As a vessel twists and winds through the reef-strewn channel to Nassau the glare of emerald water against the low green bluffs in the distance almost can transform one into the days of old New Providence. There is no sign along the route that says *beware of dangerous water,* but there should be, for the razor-sharp coral pinnacles can do considerable damage to a ship's hull. Even today, a lookout in the ratlines almost always is essential. Water depths can change from bottomless fathoms to just a few feet in a matter of seconds. Flood tides always set on the coral banks and usually run stronger between the narrow cuts. As a vessel approaches the edge of the reef the velocity of the current is most severe.

John Wilkinson was one blockade-running captain concerned with the treacherous approach to Nassau: "All of the islands are surrounded by coral reefs and shoals . . . the iron plates of the *Giraffe* would have been pierced as completely as if made of pasteboard, if she had come in contact even at low speed with those jagged coral heads."

For the most part the Bahama Islands are barren, low-lying, rocky islets. Thousands of coves and harbors are surrounded by azure water, coral reefs, and sand banks. The larger islands on which there is some degree of cultivation are densely blanketed with pine and palm forests.

Color of the water ranges from a translucent magenta in the depths offshore to a pale green close upon the beaches. Between the shore and deep water there ranges an array of beauty culminating in a variety of blue, red, brown, and green hues. Patches of coral heads and waving sea fans exist in every direction beneath the surface.

The beaches stretch out from a brilliant white to a pale pink and are composed of fine, powdery, coral sand. Even today the cruising yachtsman can sail among the Bahamas for days, anchor each evening in a secluded cove, and never see a soul.

These islands were discovered and explored in 1492 by Columbus, who made his first landing at San Salvador. In those days the Bahamas were populated by the Lucayans, who lived mostly by fishing. However, the Spaniards quickly changed the islanders' easygoing life to one of enslavement in the mines of Hispaniola.

Next came the pirates and buccaneers, and during the days of the black flag the only law in Nassau was lawlessness. Life was governed by the most notorious pirate who happened to be ashore at the time. Might was always right, and a living was made with no more difficulty than slitting a throat.

During the early eighteenth century the only trade in Nassau amounted to the pirate ships that were constantly on the go. Tavernkeepers were the principal businessmen around. Garbage and sewage rotted in the tropical heat. Whores of every nationality were in abundance. Nassau was little more than a grubby, brawling, reckless port.

A beginning at cleaning up the piratical filth-city was begun in 1718 by Woodes Rogers, a determined Englishman who had gained fame and fortune as a privateer against Spanish and French shipping. He also achieved everlasting notoriety for having rescued the marooned Alexander Selkirk, thus providing Daniel Defoe with the basis of his story *Robinson Crusoe.*

With the efforts of Woodes Rogers some semblance of law prevailed at Nassau, and English colonization progressed from that time. A few cotton and sugar plantations were established; ships stopped by to replenish their supply of fruits, vegetables, and sea turtles; hemp sisal was grown for rope products; a pearl industry was begun; and the island of New Providence became partially self-sufficient.

The first degree of affluence enjoyed in the islands came with the blockade-runners. When blockade-running began to boom, Nassau, and some of the out islands, witnessed a form of revitalization never before realized. In fact, sudden prosperity hit the sleepy town of Nassau just as it did St. George's, Bermuda.

The people of the islands took naturally to the turn of events that confronted them in 1861. Some of the inhabitants were offshoots of roving pirates from a bygone era. Others were descendants of defiant Loyalists who had come to the islands at the time of the Revolution. Many of them made their living by means of the sea alone. And all of them depended on it in one way or another.

Insecurity and risk were part of their daily lives. Adventure ran in their blood. They knew the difficult channels through hazardous coral reefs, and they could sail anything that could float. Little wonder that they jumped at the opportunity of realizing staggering amounts of money just for delivering a load of contraband cargo into blockaded Confederate ports.

Nassau was truly an *El Dorado* for blockade-runners. Its geographical advantage had been proven one hundred and fifty years earlier by rampaging freebooters who made it their headquarters. From Nassau they could prey on the Spanish galleons sailing northward with the Gulf Stream.

The island featured every advantage for a fugitive. Its harbors provided perfect ingress and egress, making it difficult to trap a ship. The thousand neighboring cays and coves made natural hiding places, and most water depths were too shallow for penetration by any deep-hulled ship-of-war.

As was the case in Bermuda, most Bahamians were sympathetic to the Southern cause—probably because of the profits they were making as a result of the war. Island commerce increased to record highs, and money was plentiful. The Nassau export house of Henry Adderley and Company did considerable trading with the Confederate States of America. Confederate agent at Nassau, Louis Heyliger, worked day and night arranging for transshipment of goods to Dixie.

Since Nassau was the chief storehouse for Confederate supplies, the majority of Southern cotton was exported with its destination Nassau. It was, without any doubt, the most convenient neutral port. The *New York Herald* reported that "Charleston or Savannah, in their palmiest days, were never so overrun with cotton as is the city of Nassau at the present time. Every available place large enough to hold half a dozen bales is crammed full and running over. It is piled up six and eight bales deep on all the wharves, vacant lots, and even on some of the lawns. It is literally 'lying around loose.'"

The lazy, sun-drenched port of Nassau, in the habit of clearing only a few ships a year from its harbor, now witnessed daily dozens of vessels riding at anchor or tied beam to beam along the wharves. Warehouses began to sag with tons of war material. Tremendous piles of crates and kegs, boxes and bales occupied every foot of dockside space.

During the day ships arrived and departed and cargoes were loaded and unloaded. At night, the streets were filled with riotous seamen and screeching wenches. Imported females vied with one another for connections with the better inns and taverns, while the common herd of mulatto girls crowded the local groghouses and bars. Barbaric orgies became a nightly event. Drinking, brawling, shouting, and cursing went on into the wee hours. Men and women slept in the streets.

James Sprunt, who sailed aboard several blockade-runners, recalled, "The wharves of Nassau were piled high with cotton during the war, and huge warehouses were stored full of supplies for the Confederacy. At times the harbor was crowded with lead-colored, short-masted, rakish-looking steamers; the streets, alive with the bustle and activity of the day, swarmed with drunken revellers at night. Almost every nationality on earth was represented there, the higher wages ashore and afloat tempting adventurers of the baser sort, and the prospect of enormous profits offering equally strong inducement to capitalists of a speculative turn. Monthly wages of a sailor on board a blockade-runner were $100 in gold, and a $50 bounty at the end of a successful trip; and this, under favorable circumstances, would be accomplished in seven days. The captains and pilots sometimes received as much as $5000. . . ."

Another contemporary account of Nassau during the days of blockade-running states, "Men wagered, gambled, drank, and seemed crazy to get rid of their money. . . . There were even times when the bank vaults would not hold all the gold, and the coins were dumped down by the bushel and guarded by soldiers."

One blockade-running sailor wrote home, "I saw two captains put up $500 each on the length of a porch. I saw men toss up twenty-dollar gold pieces on head or tail and it would be followed by a score of 'yellow boys' in five seconds. Money was almost as plenty as dirt."

In the more sumptuous hotels, officers wearing Confederate gray toasted each other (and their newly acquired lady friends) with champagne, drank to the commendable cause of the South, and saluted their hosts—the Nassau merchants, who were making fortunes overnight.

With so much going on, blockade-running skippers couldn't care less if they happened to run through a handful of gold sovereigns during the course of an evening's fun. And owners of blockade-runners could afford to lose a vessel or two after a few successful runs between Dixie and the neutral ports. Business was booming. Money was plentiful to those who dared to seek it. Old Nassau began to flourish as it did in the days of the buccaneers, and wine and women were a way of life whenever the blockade-runners were in port.

CHAPTER 17

The End of the Rainbow

"In order to evade the cruisers lying in wait off Abaco, blockade-runners were compelled to give that headland a wide berth by keeping well to the eastward of it. But in avoiding Scylla they ran the risk of striking upon Charybdis; for the dangerous reefs of Eleuthera were fatal to many vessels." *

This was to be the destiny of the blockade-runner *Cecile*. She was a prewar side-wheel steam packet ship of 360 tons that had been built in Delaware in 1857. Following her launching *Cecile* plied the waters between Charleston and Fernandina. In 1861 she was converted to a blockade-runner by John Fraser and Company of South Carolina. She had a rounded stern and iron hull. Her length was 156 feet, and she measured 29 feet across the beam. With 27 staterooms and a number of berths she could accommodate 150 passengers. In addition, the vessel could carry more than 300 bales of cotton. Under the able direction of her master, Ferdinand Peck, together with the superb seamanship of John Maffitt, who was later to become one of the most famous blockade-runners of the Confederacy, she made thirteen successful runs and generated an enormous profit for John Fraser and Company.

* John Wilkinson, *Narrative of a Blockade-Runner*, New York, 1877.

In April 1862 *Cecile* was purchased by the newly formed Importing and Exporting Company of South Carolina, of which William C. Bee and C. T. Mitchell were trustees. Her captain was James Carlin.

According to the Cotton and Captured Property Records in the National Archives, *Cecile's* first run for her new owners was on April 5, 1862, when she left Charleston for Nassau. Her cargo was 257 bales of cotton valued at $13,358. Upon reaching Nassau the sale of the cotton realized about $25,900 in Confederate currency. *Cecile's* records further illustrate the profits that were made during these times. On her return trip she brought into Charleston, among other items, six dozen ladies' spring skirts invoiced at $10.00 per dozen. They were sold at auction a few days later for $72.00 per dozen.

Such good fortune was to last only about two months, or twelve successful runs for *Cecile* and the Importing and Exporting Company of South Carolina. On June 17, 1862, the runner was loaded with a large cargo of arms and ammunitions for what was left of Sidney Johnston's army at Shiloh. The cargo included a complete battery of 8 cannon, ammunition wagons, 2000 rifles, knapsacks and harnesses, 400 barrels of powder, and a large quantity of medicines.

She had passed through Northeast Providence Channel and was maneuvering to get a line of sight on Abaco Light when the set of the current caught her. Before she could escape, *Cecile* found herself in the midst of the dreaded reefs of Abaco. The ship bumped lightly at first, rolled and groaned, then struck hard as her heavily weighted hull crashed into a large coral pinnacle. *Cecile's* entire bottom was gored open, and she sank in ten minutes. Not a single item was saved. Her crew barely escaped.

My trip to Nassau was to further research blockade-running out of that port. More significantly, I had full intentions of diving on the wreck site of famous *Cecile*. There had been very little previous salvage of the wreck, and possibilities for some captivating undersea photographs also were good. I looked forward to my mission into Nassau's past history.

Upon arrival at that sanctuary for sun-seekers I was not particularly anxious to bring any attention to my private expedition, so I endeavored to obtain the services of a reasonably inconspicuous guide. It was not long before I discovered that practically all of the native watermen profess to be specialists. With some doubt as to their actual piloting qualifications I finally selected one of the better versed guides or, perhaps I should say, "salesmen," known only as "Old Ben."

"Can you take me to the wreck of the blockade-runner *Cecile?*" I asked him, giving the general location off Abaco Light.

"Yes, sure," Old Ben said, nodding agreeably (although admitting later that the name of the wreck was unknown to him until this moment). "I have seen cannon lying on the bottom of that reef a many time while turtle fishing."

Could that be *Cecile*, I wondered? It's true that there would be cannon. They were part of the blockade-runner's cargo.

With a ten spot as a down payment, Old Ben and I made arrangements to depart early the next morning. The journey to Abaco Lighthouse, near which lay *Cecile*'s sunken wreck, involved a passage of about fifty miles. We would camp overnight at Hole in the Wall, a nearby cove on the southern end of Great Abaco, near the lighthouse, which provided a fair anchorage and exceptional fishing. This would allow plenty of time for diving, underwater photography, and exploring in general.

Morning dawned bright and clear as we left Nassau's tourist haven behind us. The sea was calm with just enough breeze to make the journey refreshing. We passed the sloops of local fishermen and several flying-bridge cruisers with shining outriggers belonging to the chartered sport fishermen. Soon the water turned a deep purple. The only noise was the creak of the rigging and the sea gently lapping against the sides of the craft.

Nobody but Old Ben talked. I was hypnotized by his accent and his remarkable knowledge of the out islands. From childhood he had been taught the lore of the sea. He talked into the morning. He was a character—a flavorsome and romantic daydreamer, a man who appreciated the wonder of nature and the vast watery world that surrounded his island paradise. He knew his way around the out islands. In fact, Old Ben and his ancestors must have been partly connected with the lore of the entire region. At least, he made it appear that way.

Old Ben's world is mostly an island called New Providence. From north to south it stretches across the azure waters of cerulean seas. His world is one of palms and pines and tourists, and scrubs and barren rocks, of barracuda, conch, and fish of every variety. He fully appreciates the vastness of his world, for within its boundary he is possessed by the passion of making a living through the pursuit of his simple way of life. But in earning a living, Old Ben is no different from many others in this world of today. He will go to market every Friday and swap a load of fish, or he will cultivate the American visitors for their almighty dollar. If he had a choice, he would admit that he prefers selling trinkets, or advice, to the tourists. But, like any other human being, there are times when he can't stand it any longer. And he turns to his first love, the sea. It just depends on the way the sun rises in the morning or how his aching back feels at night. Once out among the rolling waves in the dazzling sunlight, he becomes rejuvenated. It is here, too, that his poor man's dream of money and wealth becomes an obsession. This was how I learned of the treasure of Gorda Cay.

Gorda Cay is a small, palm-fringed isle among the Abaco group lying due north of Nassau. Its northern point is rocky and barren. Its western flank is steep-to, and consequently the island is usually visible from a seaward approach at a distance of about ten miles. There are two harbors—at opposite ends of the Cay—several beautiful white beaches, and even a private airstrip. The hues of land against sea in this area offer some of the most brilliant colors in the Bahamas.

Gorda Cay lies only about sixty miles across Northwest Providence Channel from Nassau. Its protective coral reefs are fantastically rugged and unforgettably beautiful. And although the location is extremely difficult to reach, one glance beneath the surface can hypnotize even the most experienced diver. Here, the lush tropical reefs turn almost instantly into submerged canyons. Depths vary from thirty feet to thirty fathoms, then suddenly plunge to one hundred fathoms.

Although the island is not at all near the sailing route of the Spanish plate fleets, Gorda Cay's offshore reefs mark the final resting place of a silver-laden galleon. Old Ben told me that quantities of seventy-pound silver ingots had been retrieved from the sea bottom off Gorda Cay, and it was believed that a large number still remained hidden among the coral.

Rock ballast and cannon balls imbued among the coral mark the site of the Gorda Cay treasure. Then the edge of the reef appears. Beyond it is purplish-blue emptiness from which occasionally juts a rocky crag. Large, graceful shadows with powerful fins can be seen hovering just inside the darkness of the cliff. Now and then they move outside their chasmlike home, and a ray of penetrating sunlight reveals their true identity: tigershark!

Back in 1950 a couple of Nassau businessmen discovered

one encrusted silver bar. And before them, it was reported that an American diver had recovered a few. The Nassau ingot, which today is on display by the Development Board there, was cast in 1652 at the Royal Mint in Santa Fe de Bogotá in the New Kingdom of Granada, now Bogotá, Colombia. It weighs about 72 pounds, is in excellent condition, and contains about 93.5 percent pure silver, the remainder being copper. The bar of silver was identified as having originated at the royal foundry in Bogotá and is believed to be the personal property of His Majesty King Philip IV (1621–1665). The value of the find ranges upward from $20,000.

The *Miami Herald* reported the treasure on June 18, 1952, stating that the ingot was recovered "from the solid ocean floor, near Gorda Cay, a short distance from where the ocean drops off to great depths. If it was a treasure ship, there is a king's ransom in the area, although it may be too deep for recovery. Such ships would carry not less than $2,000,000, and records indicate some of them carried as high as $10,000,000."

Old Ben's story was fantastic. Although it had the familiar tone of so many tales of sunken treasure, I could not help but be intrigued. He knew the details well, and it was apparent that he had dreamed for a long time of discovering for himself a silver bar or two. I wanted to believe him.

We were then in the middle of the channel, about halfway between Nassau and our destination, the wreck of the historic blockade-runner *Cecile*. For a long while neither of us spoke. As I think back now in retrospect I'm sure that was just the way Old Ben had planned it.

Finally, the silence was broken. "How far is it to this place, Gorda Cay?" I asked.

Old Ben looked up, grinning slyly. " 'Bout the same distance as we're presently headed."

"Is there a spot to anchor and camp?" I inquired.

"Better even than Hole in the Wall," said he. "Hole in the Wall is one bad place to be caught in a southerly. Sometimes there is a difficult westerly set, too." Old Ben hesitated, then glanced at me again, his dark eyes flashing. "Gorda Cay is beautiful," he added.

It was afternoon when we arrived off Gorda Cay. And it took Old Ben a long time to find the "wreck site." Finally we dropped anchor over a pile of ballast and coral conglomerate.

"This is the spot," he said. "It is hard to find because there is very little left of the wreck."

I grabbed a mask and snorkel and swam around the area. The water was shallow and gin-clear. Not far away, the reef stopped, dropping off into unknown depths. The coral formations were wild and beautiful. Myriad brightly colored fish surrounded me. I had never seen anything like it.

Returning to the sloop I said to Old Ben, "You were right, Gorda Cay is truly beautiful. There is treasure all around us. But I did not see any silver."

He laughed and motioned toward the edge of the reef. "I think it would be best to search near the ledge. If the ship was lost during a hurricane, part of her hull grounded here, where she broke up. But when the eye passed over, and the winds reversed, the other portion of the vessel would have been blown back into the deep water over there."

I donned one of the few tanks of compressed air and moved beneath the surface in the direction of Old Ben's gesture. As I swam along slowly looking over the reef bottom, the entire ocean seemed to open up and swallow me. Deeper and deeper I went, beyond the pile of ballast and coral-covered cannon balls. Still there was no bottom. Far above me the surface of the water looked like a mirrored ceiling. I could no longer see the shadow of Old Ben's boat.

Barracuda that hung like silent sentinels above a lofty crag one hundred feet away seemed to signal, "The galleon is here." Breathtaking formations of unusual coral and finger sponge that zigzagged out of sight into an abyss beyond seemed to say, "The silver is over here." A playful school of iridescent mackerel darting back and forth seemed to communicate, "Follow me, it is this way."

In this amazing undersea oasis, overlooking fantastic endlessness, inhabited by colossal beauty that exists under colossal tides—any man who dares to belong, to understand and become a part of such an intriguing environment, could have only colossal dreams. And the more I followed the gestures of the barracuda or the signs of the swift mackerel, the more significant became my quest for riches, the more I appreciated the interminable dream of Old Ben.

At the end of the day's hard diving we shifted the boat to shore, watching the amber spectrum of sunset dissolve slowly over the quiet horizon. In the same direction, the galleon of silver waited. The serenity and beauty of Old Ben's world had me in a daze. As we settled down that evening I must have known that it would take many days of searching to find the treasure of Gorda Cay, if there was a treasure. And, yet, the challenge of something that will always be unexplainable lured us back again the next morning—back to the venerable cliffs surrounded by blue; back to the tons of sand covering a hidden trail of ballast; back to the labyrinthian formations of coral and sea fans whose hypnotic charm I was beginning to understand.

We did not find the silver of Gorda Cay. And it is doubtful that there is any treasure left on the same reef where the Nassau ingot was discovered. The rest of the wreck probably lies beyond the edge of the coral cliff in deep water, protected by such physiological factors as nitrogen narcosis and compressed air hazards. Someday, perhaps, it will be found and salvaged. However, the problems of diving here are many. Without an air compressor, scuba diving is limited. Only brief explorations can be accomplished with a snorkel; and without proper supplies and equipment, sustained effort underwater is difficult.

The environment, though, is worth the trip. The fishing is extraordinary. And being in the out islands is like being in another world.

On the way back, my temporary case of "treasure fever" broke. I was dismayed that the end of the rainbow had lured me away from my primary objective, the wreck of the *Cecile*. The real purpose of my trip had gone to waste.

It must have been a similar disillusionment that crushed the hopes of the Nassau speculators who were engaged in the contraband trade a hundred years earlier. As we neared Nassau's colorful harbor I recalled coincidentally the comments of Captain John Wilkinson as he headed his sleek steamer, *Chameleon*, into that same harbor on his last voyage as a Confederate blockade-runner: "It was too evident that the end was near. The speculators in Nassau saw that the bottom had fallen out, and all of them were in the depths of despair. Some of them, it is true, had risen from the desperately hazardous game with large gains, but the majority had staked their all and lost it; and even the fortunate ones had contracted a thirst for rash ventures."

But Old Ben was in good spirits. This was just another expedition toward ultimate conquest as far as he was concerned. The journey had invigorated him. His hopes and dreams were rekindled.

However, Old Ben's hopes did not evolve solely around his secret of the galleon. Somewhere in his indescribable world of fish, water, and island lore, he had found the answer to living his way of life to the fullest. And he could well afford to wait another day to reap his reward of silver from the bottom of the sea. Old Ben preferred a campfire on a moonlit cove to the night life of the city. And what better way was there to earn a dollar than floating on the sea's calm surface with the sun on his back, watching the contour of the reef for a shipwreck of the past?

Our small vessel eased into the crowded harbor. After a few moments of maneuvering past the luxurious yachts and cruisers lying side by side and at anchor, we made our way to a not-so-luxurious slip.

Old Ben was quiet now. There was an expression of serenity on his face as he went about the routine of making his craft secure. Gathering my gear, I shoved fins, mask, and scuba regulator into the sea bag.

Taking one final look around, I left the boat. Old Ben heaved the equipment up to the dock. Still, he was silent.

Grubbing in my dungaree pocket I pulled out a small wad of bills and paid the balance of his fee. His eyes lit up at the sight of the money, and he came to life. Immediately he assumed a role of exuberance.

"When do you leave?" he asked.

"Early in the morning," I responded.

"Oh," said he, staring out across the emerald water.

I looked around also. It was cocktail time. The after decks of any number of yachts could be seen occupied by gaily attired ladies and gentlemen. A breeze ruffled the water, and the smell of the sea and activity of the city emanated all around.

Old Ben hopped up on the dock, following me to the edge of the wharf.

Picking up my gear I turned to him. "Thanks, Captain," I murmured. "It was a memorable trip."

He looked at me with his dark eyes dancing. Then, with outstretched hand, he said confidently, "We need more time to work the galleon wreck. And more tanks of air, and more diving equipment . . ." Old Ben paused, "On your next visit," he said, "I will surely take you to the blockade runner *Cecile*. She lies near Pirate Rock . . . where Blackbeard's gold is buried."

VI

WHAT THE SANDS
UNCOVER

"All approaches to Wilmington are paved as thickly with valuables as a certain place is said to be with good intentions."

CHAPTER 18

Rebel Relics

Stand on the beach anywhere along the coast near Wilmington or Charleston. Look beyond the breaking surf, out over the rolling waves, and reflect upon the history written within your line of sight. There, more than a century ago, blockade-runners stranded, passed safely, or were captured or destroyed. In these very waters a small group of men and ships endeavored to save the Confederacy by bringing to her ports much needed supplies.

But deeply imbedded in the sands of the Carolinas lies the climax to the story of the blockade-runners. Here, hidden for posterity, are clues to the past history of many of these proud ships.

The sand-covered cargoes of the Confederate-bound runners are now nothing more than rusty remnants of a century-old epoch. Having been exposed to more than a hundred years of waves, wind, tides, and the chemical action of the sea, most of the hardware which the South awaited with anxiety has now deteriorated beyond recognition, or corroded beyond repair.

No matter what the reader's interest—whether he be a scuba diver, historian, or merely seeking armchair adventure—he should appreciate the imperishable significance of these lost ships, for within their rusting hulls lie relics of a bygone era, immortal links in the chain of history, or perhaps the excitement of discovery, of which most men only dream.

Although shifting sands hide most of the wrecked blockade-runners, occasionally strong tides and storms uncover their remains. Beachcombers and scuba divers who watch for heavy tides and locate a lost runner often recover valuable relics. Heavy, bulk-type cargo such as lead ingots, projectiles, and encrusted muskets can be found on the bottom, together with smaller artifacts of a general nature.

However, diving on these wrecks is not an undertaking for just an average scuba diver. Visibility beneath the surface often is very poor. Jagged sections of wreckage may be present, particularly if the ship was heavily fired upon at the time of sinking. Wave ground swells coupled with strong currents add to the diver's dilemma.

Although most of the sunken wooden-hulled sailing vessels have long since decayed, remains of iron steamers are amazingly well intact. Since most of the blockade-runners ran aground or were beached and sank within several hundred yards of the shore, their wrecks are in shallow water.

On days when water visibility is good, the shadows of sunken hulks can be spotted, as can the swirl of "boilers" and discolored or disturbed water area, over many of the shipwrecks. But it takes a thorough knowledge of the sea and an understanding of the science of navigation to locate a sunken blockade-runner, or any other type of shipwreck, for that matter. Murky water, an occasional shark, and lack of reliable information are the reasons many of the wrecked blockade-runners have not been salvaged or discovered.

The Carolina coasts are, of course, not the only regions in which blockade-runners were lost. Every Southern state bordering on the sea can claim at least a few.

Activities of blockade-runners into Gulf of Mexico ports

also were significant. A fantastic number of arms as well as clothing and food were imported through Gulf ports. However, most of the runners that plied these waters were relatively small sailing vessels which, because of their light draft, were the principal type of ships operating successfully in this spacious area. Hundreds of these blockade-running sailing vessels were captured by Yankee cruisers on patrol. Many more were beached in shallow water, burned, and destroyed.

There were a few distinguished steamers that successfully ran the blockade in the Gulf of Mexico before their careers ended forever. The British steamer *Denbigh*, for instance, accomplished more than two dozen successful runs during the latter part of the war before being chased ashore off Galveston in May 1865. The steamer *Havana* also made profitable contributions to the Southern cause in the Gulf area before being wrecked and burned at Dead Man's Bay in June of 1862. The 200-ton blockade-running steamer *Little Lila* was destroyed near the mouth of the Suwanee River in February of 1864 after an outstanding career. In September of 1863 the *Fox* was set on fire by her owner near Pascagoula, Mississippi, in order to keep the ship from being captured. The *Will O' the Wisp* was sunk and burned near Galveston in February of 1865 after an outstanding career. And there were others.

History has given only casual mention to the activities of the gallant blockade-runners, and few historians have referred to the significant contribution these men and ships made to the Confederate cause. Today, however, many of these proud steamers stand as monuments beneath the sea. Cloaked in the grandeur of marine life, their hulks offer a timeworn remembrance of the days of the Yankee blockade and of those who dared to test it.

The following pages discuss sequential events involving the fate of a number of blockade-runners not covered elsewhere in this book. And although there were many more ships destroyed while attempting to run the blockade, the following accounts concern only those vessels whose total destruction was momentous, and whose deeds would qualify them, above all, for the June 7, 1863, *Wilmington Daily Journal* definition of a blockade-runner:

"The men who run the blockade have to be men who can stand fire without returning it. It is a business in which every man takes his life in his hands, and he so understands it. An ordinarily brave man has no business on a blockade-runner. He who makes a success of it is obliged to have the cunning of a fox, the patience of a Job, and the bravery of a Spartan warrior. The runners must not be armed and must not resist; they must simply be cool and quick and watchful and, for the rest, trust to God and their good ship to deliver them safely to their friends."

MODERN GREECE
June 27, 1862
Richmond Is Saved After Seven Sanguinary Days

The loss of the *Modern Greece* was one of the first great blockade-running disasters. She was one of the largest vessels to attempt to run the blockade and was heavily laden with munitions and war materials. Ironically, her final resting place was only a relatively few yards from her final destination.

The *Modern Greece* was a slate-colored, schooner-rigged, propeller steamer of approximately 1000 tons. Loaded with a hull full of gunpowder, more than a half-dozen Whitworth rifled cannon, clothing, and liquors, she had slipped through the line of gunboats and was approaching the Federal Point Batteries of Fort Fisher. The weather was thick and visibility was zero. As the blockade-runner felt her way toward the mouth of New Inlet she ran right into the U.S.S. *Cambridge*, which immediately opened fire.

The U.S.S. *Stars and Stripes* also joined in the bombardment, striking the fugitive nine times. There being no sea room in which to maneuver, and seeing that she was cut off, the *Modern Greece* turned her bow toward the beach and ran aground.

After her crew escaped, Confederate batteries opened fire on the derelict in an effort to sink her and prevent the Federals from salvaging the cargo. The superior range of Fort Fisher's guns forced the Union fleet to retreat and allowed the Confederates an opportunity to salvage six of the rifled cannon, 500 stands of arms, and a large amount of powder and clothing.

However, the greater portion of the runner's cargo was never salvaged. A Confederate report stated that 7000 Enfield muskets were left aboard, as well as four brass field artillery pieces. In 1962, a hundred years later, Navy divers assisted the North Carolina Department of Archives and History in recovering artifacts for the Fort Fisher Museum. Scores of encrusted British rifles were brought to the surface together with numerous twelve-pound projectiles for the Whitworth gun. Tons of lead and tin ingots also were salvaged, as well as thousands of bullets, eating utensils, Bowie knives, carpenter tools, medical kits, and leather shoes.

The remains of the *Modern Greece* lie in about 40 feet of water, 200 yards offshore. Scuba divers interested in exploring this wreck should coordinate their activities with the Fort Fisher authorities. More than one salvage firm already has locked horns with state officials by attempting salvage without permission. The state of North Carolina claims title to all Civil War wrecks. Many scuba divers, however, take opposite views. They contend that the state abandoned the sunken ships at the end of the Civil War and has no right to claim them now. So far, the state's word has prevailed.

SOPHIA
June 27, 1862
Confederates Dig in at Fredericksburg

The *Sophia* was a 375-ton British bark out of Liverpool. She had made two previously successful trips through the blockade, carrying large shipments of arms and supplies into Wilmington. Her captain, James Forbes, had earned quite a name for himself, considering *Sophia*'s relative slowness as a sailing vessel.

While loaded with a valuable cargo including three brass rifled fieldpieces, small arms, ammunition, gun carriages, salt, saltpeter, and soda ash, the *Sophia* was discovered by the U.S.S. *Daylight* about four miles to the south of Masonboro Inlet.

Seeing escape impossible Captain Forbes headed the bark straight for the beach, hoping to save some of the cargo. However, there was little time and the surf was heavy. Transfers of cargo would be difficult, so the white flag was run up.

The *Daylight* apparently refused to recognize the signal of surrender as she fired shell after shell at the grounded vessel. Then, seeing the crew of the blockade-runner heading for shore, the *Daylight* lowered her own boats in an effort to stop them.

However, each of the *Daylight*'s small boats were caught broadside to the breakers. The embarrassed Yankees lost three officers, three boats, and eighteen men, all of whom were captured as they washed up on the beach.

Union reports stated that "the bark and cargo . . . were totally destroyed." The main and mizzen masts had "gone by the board," and the "shrouds and backstays to the foremast, cut." The ship was burned to the water's edge.

GEORGIANA
March 19, 1863
Vicksburg Braces for a Fight

The U.S. Consul at Teneriffe wrote, on February 13, 1863:

"English screw steamer *Georgiana* left this port yesterday for Nassau. From her appearance and the circumstances of her officers wearing gold lace on their caps, coupled with the description of her in the *London American* of Jan. 28, I fear that she is an armed vessel, intended for a cruiser."

The Consul at Nassau wrote, on February 27, 1863: ". . . Also arrived the brig-rigged iron propeller *Georgiana*, another confederate to the pirate *Alabama*. . . . These vessels . . . are a formidable addition to the rebel fleet."

Georgiana was a powerful steamer of 407 tons and 150 horsepower. She had two masts with yards on both, one stack forward, and was brig-rigged.

Her captain was A. B. Davidson, a retired British Naval officer. Early in the morning of March 19, 1863, she attempted to run into Charleston through Maffitt's Channel and was spotted by Acting Master J. Baker aboard the U.S. yacht *America*, which fired into her. The *America's* shots alerted the nearby gunboat, U.S.S. *Wissahickon*. Lieutenant-Commander John L. Davis acted promptly, placing the *Wissahickon* directly in front of the fast approaching blockade-runner. He immediately launched a heavy fire.

Seeing all hope of escape impossible, skipper Davidson stopped the *Georgiana* and showed a light, making known to the gunboat his intentions of surrendering. However, after the *Wissahickon* ceased firing, *Georgiana* changed her heading northward and rang up full speed for the beach. After running aground, she again displayed her white light, and the gunboat ceased firing. The *Georgiana*, loaded with valuable cargo for which the Confederates were in desperate need, was left where she stranded about two miles to the eastward of Breach Inlet, three quarters of a mile off-shore.

Lieutenant Davis immediately dispatched boats under the command of Lieutenant S. Casey with orders for all on board to be brought back to the *Wissahickon*. But when Mr. Casey reached the stranded runner, her crew had vanished in their boats. There was no trace of the Rebel vessel's log book or her cargo manifest. Apparently, every means was taken to make sure the *Georgiana* would not be floated by her captors, for the vessel was found to have fourteen feet of water in her hold.

Having exhausted their efforts to float the blockade-runner, the Yankees recovered as much cargo as they could during the night and, just at daylight, set the *Georgiana* on fire. She burned slowly for several days, which resulted in several terrific explosions. A heavy sea ran for two days, preventing any further salvage. The Rebel loss was not to become a Yankee gain, as the only items reported in official dispatches as salvaged were 8 Enfield rifles, 9 bayonets, 8 battle-axes, 1 lead and line, 10 pounds of glue, 5 small jars of preserves, 12 gilt buttons, and 19 sabers.

Had the Union officers who boarded the *Georgiana* known the nature of her cargo, they would have made more extensive efforts at salvage. She was, in fact, one of the heaviest laden vessels to try to enter Charleston. The vessel was pierced for 14 guns and was to be fitted out as a Confederate cruiser. She carried 140 well-trained men, together with "an armament of guns and gun carriages in her hold." In addition, she was loaded with great quantities of rifled guns, projectiles, Enfield rifles, powder, and many articles of assorted merchandise.

Rear Admiral S. F. DuPont made known his pleasure over this Northern conquest, stating, "I was aware of the character of this vessel, and consider her capture of the utmost importance." He also mentioned at a later date that it was "impossible to secure any of the valuable part of her cargo before she was set on fire by our vessels."

The next night a boat was captured with a sergeant and eight soldiers of the Confederate Army who were trying to get out to the *Georgiana* but became lost in the dark. They reported that they had been sent to the runner "to look after her."

Three men from Liverpool who were passengers aboard the derelict made it safely to the west end of Sullivan's Island, where they were questioned at the signal station. They confirmed the value of the steamer, saying that she had a very large amount of ordnance stores and assorted merchandise of considerable worth.

STONEWALL JACKSON
April 11, 1863
Fake Torpedoes in Charleston Harbor Thwart Union Attack

The *Stonewall Jackson* (formerly the *Leopard*) was a side-wheel steamer of 862 tons. She was running an extremely valuable cargo of munitions and supplies from Nassau. The runner was discovered by four Union blockaders late in the evening as she was trying to sneak through the North Channel for Charleston. With her paddle wheels churning up the sea, the blockade-runner tried for an hour to outdistance her pursuers. But she could not outrun the Yankee guns, and several shells struck her hull below the waterline. Captain Black, finding escape impossible, decided to beach his vessel, hoping to save at least a portion of the runner's badly needed cargo. The ship was grounded off Long Island. After setting the *Stonewall Jackson* on fire about daylight of the twelfth, the crew and passengers, numbering fifty-four in all, took to the boats. They headed for Sullivan's Island, about a mile and a half down the coast, and found shelter at Battery Marshall.

This blockade-runner had made eight previously successful round trips. Her loss on this ninth run was indeed unfortunate, as all cargo went up in flames. "Very little was
saved excepting the mail and the passenger's effects." Her
cargo consisted of several pieces of field artillery, 200 barrels of saltpeter, 40,000 army shoes, and a large assortment
of merchandise.

The *Stonewall Jackson* was reported a complete loss,
having "burned to the water's edge in sight of the Yankees
. . . about one-half mile from the beach and one and a half
miles from the Breach Inlet batteries."

Captain Charles T. Haskell, Jr., commanding Battery
Marshall, later said that the blockade-runner need not have
been burned, since it was near enough to have been protected by his guns. Thus ended the career of another Rebel
runner.

RUBY
June 11, 1863
Lee Pushes Toward Pennsylvania

The day of June 11, 1863, had just begun when, shortly
after midnight, the Federal gunboats *Memphis*, *Stettin*, and
Ottawa spotted a darkened vessel hauling into Lawford
Channel toward Charleston Harbor. All three cruisers gave
chase, firing at the silhouette while she was within range.
At daylight the low-slung blockade-runner was discovered
onshore at the northern part of Folly Island, burning fore
and aft. She appeared to be well grounded, for she stood
practically high and dry at low water.

Commodore Turner, of the U.S.S. *New Ironsides*, reported that she was "a very large steamer with side wheels"
and "doubtless was run ashore in a sinking condition to save
her from sinking in the channel."

Later in the morning, boats were launched from the
Powhatan and *Sebago* to try to put out the fire and refloat

the vessel. However, as they approached the beach they received heavy fire from the batteries at the lower end of Morris Island and were forced to retreat farther offshore.

The following evening the Yankees succeeded in getting a couple of men on board the blockade-runner. They were in hopes that under the cover of night they could retrieve much of the valuable cargo. But they were discovered the next day by the Confederates, who opened a sharp fire on the wreck and terrorized the Union sailors who had slipped aboard the hulk. It was all the Yankees could do to scramble off the wreck and flee for their lives.

Several days later it became known that the wrecked vessel was none other than the notorious blockade-runner *Ruby*, which had made numerous trips in and out of Charleston. Every gunboat commander along the coast had her listed on their "most wanted" sheet.

Ruby was a 400-ton iron, paddle-wheel steamer. She was schooner-rigged, with two smokestacks (one forward of the wheelhouse and the other in line with the after section of her paddles). She carried a crew of twenty-two, drew seven feet of water, was very long and low, and could attain unbelievable speed. The vessel had left Havana on June 2, 1863, before having the misfortune of being fired upon and struck by the blockaders. *Ruby* ran ashore on Folly Island near Lighthouse Inlet. The Confederates subsequently dismantled much of her machinery. In fact, her iron plates were removed and used for sandbag lining braces. Confederate soldiers also carried most of her supplies to shore, where they divided the loot.

HEBE
August 18, 1863
Gettysburg Is Over and Vicksburg Has Fallen

The *Hebe* was a fast, double-screw, Crenshaw steamer that had made two highly successful trips through the Yankee blockade. Early in the morning of August 18, 1863, she was trying for her third successful run as she steamed southward toward New Inlet and the safety of Fort Fisher. Crammed into her hold was a cargo of coffee, medicine, and clothing.

When about halfway between Fort Fisher and Mason-boro Inlet, the blockade-runner's black smoke was noticed by an alert watch of the U.S.S. *Niphon*. As the gunboat gained on the small steamer, *Hebe*'s skipper acted by turn-ing her head toward the beach, purposely running the ves-sel aground. The crew took to the boats and reached shore safely through heavy surf.

Although a thirty-knot northeaster was blowing, the commander of the *Niphon* ordered a boatload of Union sailors to the stranded runner to set her on fire. This they successfully accomplished. But upon returning to their small boat, they found it had been swamped and sunk. Con-siderable panic prevailed as the Federal sailors raced around the blockade-runner trying to extinguish the fires they had just started.

Other boats were sent by the *Niphon* to rescue the sail-ors, but these either capsized or were driven ashore by the heavy seas. The Confederates on the beach were delighted over the Yankees' predicament. They welcomed the half-drowned Union sailors as each one was washed upon the beach and taken prisoner.

Shortly afterward the Confederates located two Whit-worth guns just behind the sand dunes at the scene of the action. These guns inflicted assorted damage on the *Niphon* cruising offshore.

However, to the horror of the stranded Union sailors still aboard the wrecked *Hebe*, their mother ship began shelling the blockade-runner. After a couple of rounds the sailors got the message and jumped into the sea, swam ashore, and were captured. Twice the *Hebe* was on fire from the constant shelling, and twice the flames were extinguished by the heavy seas rolling over the grounded vessel. The steady firing from the Whitworths in the dunes, the loss of three boats and fifteen men with equipment, and the howling northeaster caused the Yankees to withdraw from the scene.

Two days later, six Federal gunboats were ordered to the *Hebe* to destroy the wreck completely and prevent any further salvage. As the first warship approached within 600 yards of the *Hebe*, the Whitworths on the beach opened fire. The Confederate shells found their mark on the U.S.S. *Minnesota*, which promptly returned the fire. Unnoticed by the Rebels, however, was a landing party from another gunboat further down the beach. As the U.S. ships *Minnesota* and *James Adger* bombarded the Whitworth position, the Union landing party came down upon the Whitworth crew and disabled the Confederate guns. With his small party killed or wounded, Captain Munn in charge of the Whitworths "was compelled to fall back under a heavy enfilade fire toward Fort Fisher, with the loss of his guns."

The loss of the Whitworths was a serious one to the Confederates defending the area. The Whitworth long-range firepower had saved dozens of blockade-runners that were being closely pursued by gunboats. But the cost of their capture was also expensive to the Yankees. *Official Records* indicate that a total of 335 shell and shot was fired at the Confederate gun position on the date of the skirmish.

The *Wilmington Daily Journal* reported afterward that "the houses, and fences, and woods in the neighborhood were riddled with shot and shell. Four shots passed through Mr. James Burris' house. The hills around the wreck are furrowed like a ploughed field. . . ."

DOURO
October 11, 1863
Confederate Submarine David *Drives Spar Torpedo into* U.S.S. New Ironsides

The *Douro* was a 180-ton iron-screw steamer. With a crew of twenty-two she had run the blockade three times successfully before being captured in March of 1863 by the U.S.S. *Quaker City*. The ship had been condemned, sold as a prize, taken to Nassau, and again placed in the blockade-running trade under the same name.

After making three more profitable trips into Wilmington, the little runner was loaded with cotton, tobacco, turpentine, and resin owned by the Confederate government. She had passed through New Inlet about nine thirty in the evening when, just after crossing the bar, she was sighted by an alert watch of the U.S.S. *Nansemond*.

The chase began with the *Douro* traveling in only two and a half fathoms of water. The *Nansemond* pressed for all available steam in an effort to place herself between the fleeing fugitive and the beach. The warship was unable to cut off the runner, however, and the *Douro* began to pull ahead of the *Nansemond*.

But on this particular evening fate was against the Rebels. *Douro* ran aground at full speed. The blockade-runner was quickly boarded by the Federals, who took five prisoners. However, *Douro*'s captain, pilot, and most of her crew escaped.

Members of the *Nansemond*'s crew tried to refloat the stranded runner but were unsuccessful. By daybreak the vessel was set on fire, and much of her superstructure burned to the water's edge. The location of the wreck of the *Douro* is near the surf zone above Fort Fisher, just north of the remains of the *Hebe*. The hulk of the blockade-runner *Venus* also is close by.

VENUS
October 21, 1863
The Blockade Noose Tightens

The *Venus* was an unusually large British steamer that was sheathed completely with iron, drew eight feet of water, and was reported to have had extremely fine engines. She was 265 feet in length and possessed a capacity of 1000 tons. The ship carried a crew of twenty-three and had been extremely profitable, having made approximately a dozen successful penetrations of the Federal blockade.

Having departed from Nassau several days earlier, the *Venus* was discovered by the U.S. ships *Nansemond* and *Niphon* at midnight as the runner was heading for New Inlet at a speed of fourteen knots. The warships opened a heavy fire. One of the first shots caved in an iron plate near the waterline of the blockade-runner, causing her to ship water in large quantities. Another shot exploded in her wardroom, and another forward, killing one of the crew.

Seeing that his vessel was in danger of sinking, the skipper of the *Venus*, Captain Charles Murray, headed the runner toward the beach and ran aground. Because of the speed at which she was traveling, Yankee crews were unable to refloat the *Venus*. Instead they blew up her boilers, riddled her hull with shot, and set the derelict on fire. "Nothing is left but her iron hull, she is a complete wreck . . . ," was the official report.

Twenty-three crew members of the blockade-runner were captured before they could lower her lifeboat. The ship's papers also were taken by the Unionists, some gold was discovered, and other miscellaneous articles were salvaged.

The cargo manifest listed drugs, lead, dry goods, bacon and coffee, guns and ammunition, and a quantity of rum. In addition, the *Venus* was reported to be hauling a model of "the new railway," although the location of the proposed railway was not known.

The *Venus* ran aground above New Inlet from one to two miles north of Gatlin's battery between Flag Pond Hill and Dick's Bay. Ninety-seven shells were fired into her by the *Niphon* and unestimated amounts by the *Nansemond*.

Today the location of the wreck is known, and the vessel's hull can be found fairly intact. Tons of lead remain inside her, as do handsome pieces of crockery bearing the ship's name.

ANTONICA
December 20, 1863
Battle Above the Clouds Breaks the Army of Tennessee

One of the most successful blockade-runners was the 563-ton *Antonica*, also known as the *Herald*. She was captained by an old pro, W. F. Adair, out of Charleston.

The ship was attempting to bring a cargo of liquor, dry goods, general provisions, and clothing into Wilmington when she found herself in the midst of the Union fleet. The runner had outwitted half a dozen warships when, on the western side of Frying Pan Shoals, she made a daring decision to try to pass *inshore* of the U.S.S. *Governor Buckingham*. Steering through the line of shoals her luck ran out, and the *Antonica* stranded at three o'clock in the morning. Captain Adair and his crew took to their boats, but were fired upon by the Union warship and surrendered. All forty-two were taken prisoner.

Union boarding parties made strenuous efforts to free the stranded runner. However, since the *Antonica* had grounded at high tide, they were unable to get her off. Several days later she was reported to be bilged and broken across her bottom. Part of the blockade-runner's cargo was salvaged by the Yankees. Also some $1200 was found on board.

Today the remains of this famous ship are buried in the sand about three and a half miles due south of Cape Fear.

VESTA
January 11, 1864
A Lot of Rebel Land Is Lost in the West

The *Vesta* was an iron, double-propeller steamer of about 500 tons. *Official Records* report the location of this shipwreck as being "four miles below and to the westward of Tubb's Inlet." Today, the Vesta Fishing Pier at Sunset Beach stretches seaward directly over the boiler of this blockade-runner. Many species of fish frequent the environs of her rusting hulk. At the time of sinking she carried thousands of pairs of shoes, blankets, clothing (including a new uniform for Robert E. Lee), and reams of paper and stationery. All cargo was consumed by flames as the ship burned for hours.

A correspondent for the *Richmond Dispatch* was returning from Europe aboard *Vesta*, having joined the ship at Bermuda. He witnessed the grounding of the blockade-runner and blamed the loss of the vessel on the ship's officers. "Captain Eustace got falling down drunk." The first mate remained sober enough to take a sun sight—"But he was too drunk to plot it." The pilot had to be assisted on deck "from the liquor locker," and was unable to determine the course to be steered. Thus ended the life of another blockade-runner. After striking the shoals during the night, *Vesta*'s crew set the ship afire.

The next morning vessels of the blockading fleet spotted the smoke of the burning runner. U.S.S. *Aries* investigated and found the "whole starboard side opened and several plates split . . . she had five feet of water in her." The *Vesta* was left burning "fore and aft." There was no report of salvage other than two anchors.

RANGER
January 11, 1864
Few Confederate Ports Are Now Open

The *Ranger* left Newcastle, England, on November 11, 1863, bound for Bermuda. She stopped at Teneriffe, and finally arrived at Bermuda on December 8, 1863. She left that place on January 6, 1864, making the Carolina coast on January 10. Since the weather was bad and the blockading fleet had extinguished the Frying Pan Shoals lightship, she put to shore about five miles northeast of Murrell's Inlet to ascertain her position and, once determined, landed her passengers and baggage. Then, at midnight, January 11, the *Ranger* got under way again, running along the coast for the bar near Fort Caswell. When she was eight miles from the fort, a number of Union warships were sighted, including the *Minnesota, Daylight, Governor Buckingham,* and *Aries,* causing the "obviously nervous" pilot to steer the *Ranger* inshore onto the breakers. After setting her afire, Lieutenant George W. Gift, master, abandoned the vessel with his crew. She was discovered at daybreak. The Yankees attempted to get the *Ranger* off the shoals, but the blockade-runner was completely enfiladed by fire from Confederate sharpshooters in the sand hills.

Scuba divers are recovering handsome relics from the remains of the *Ranger*. She lies in about 20 feet of water about 200 yards offshore of Holden Beach, North Carolina. On days of good visibility the entire outline of her hull can be seen from the air. During very low tides "boilers" are visible around a portion of the uppermost part of the wreck. At the time of this writing, thousands of Austrian rifles still remain in the bottom of the *Ranger*'s hull covered with sand. The muskets are packed in crates containing twenty-four guns each together with bayonets. After a thorough soaking in fresh water many of the wooden stocks can be restored by generous coatings of linseed oil. The metal bay-onets can be preserved by soaking them in a bath of sodium hydroxide for about two months and then thoroughly cov-ering the exposed surface with liquid plastic or wax.

WILD DARRELL
February 2, 1864
Confederate Commerce Raiders Report Successful Cruises

The *Wild Darrell* was a double-stacked, paddle-wheel steamer of about 440 tons. She had left Nassau at the end of January and was discovered at noon "in about the par-allel of Topsail Inlet."

Apparently the blockade-runner had accidentally stranded while taking refuge in the inlet. Half her cargo of shoes, blankets, and provisions had been thrown upon the beach. The estimated value was $200,000.

The U.S.S. *Sassacus* began firing on the runner, causing the *Darrell's* crew to head for the dunes. For the next two days the Federals attempted to free the stranded ship. Their efforts being unsuccessful the blockade-runner was set afire and then shelled.

Captain Row of the *Sassacus* reported "not half of her cargo had been thrown overboard and the rest, which I deemed very valuable merchandise, was consumed with the vessel." Captain Crosby of the U.S.S. *Florida* stated, "I have a case of musket caps (percussion), taken from the *Wild Darrell*, containing 270,000 caps."

Today the ruins of the *Wild Darrell* are well sanded in. However, anyone ambitious enough to search for a trace of her rusting relics may well stumble upon fragments of the Spanish galleon *El Salvador* which went down more than a hundred years earlier in the same vicinity. The Span-ish ship also had a cargo of $200,000, but most of it was in silver.

DEE
February 6, 1864

Ever Hopeful Rebs Prepare for Another Spring

The *Dee* was a fast blockade-runner of some 200 tons that was loaded with guns and ammunition for the Rebel Army. She carried also a large number of heavy lead ingots to be melted down for bullets. Having made one previously successful run, the ship was inward bound and racing parallel with the shore toward New Inlet. When in the vicinity of Masonboro Inlet, the blockade-runner struck a shoal of sand and was unable to free herself. Several hundred bars of lead were thrown over the starboard side in a frantic effort to lighten the load. She was soon sighted by Union warships, whose shells ended any Confederate hopes at salvage. The ship was completely destroyed. Today the pile of lead is still alongside the *Dee's* rusting hull.

An interesting, but tragic, article in the *Wilmington Journal* of April 16, 1864, covers an incident related to the loss of the *Dee*. "Some weeks ago the steamer *Dee* was beached opposite Mr. Thomas Hansley's plantation, where she was shelled by the enemy, some of the shells coming over and burying themselves in the land. A few days since, the Negroes at work in Mr. Hansley's fields ploughed up one of these shells from which they removed the cap or fuse, and on Tuesday last Mr. William Banton, a relation of Mr. Hansley's, determined on trying the shell to see if it would explode, applying a lighted twig or dry branch. . . . The shell did explode, injuring him terribly, if not fatally. Dr. Thomas . . . had to amputate his right foot near the instep and his left leg just below the knee. His recovery must be regarded as very doubtful."

FANNY AND JENNY
February 10, 1864
Confederate Submarine Hunley *Sinks U.S.S.* Housatonic *off Charleston*

This ship had a tremendously interesting career as a blockade-runner. She was originally named *Scotia* and had made four or five successful round trips into and out of Confederate ports. However, she was captured in October of 1862 off South Carolina and turned over to the Prize Court. Unknown to the Federals, she was purchased by a group of Confederates, renamed *Fanny and Jenny*, and again placed in active blockade-running.*

The *Fanny and Jenny* was a two-stack, side-wheel steamer capable of making thirteen knots. She had left Nassau on February 5, 1864, under the command of the famous Louis Coxetter. The night of February 9 saw the runner approaching Wilmington in heavy seas. Her pilot, by the name of Burrows (or Burroughs), had previously served the interests of the Union Navy, but had deserted. On this particular evening it was necessary for him to stop the ship several times in order to determine his position. Dawn caught him still trying to find New Inlet. At 6:00 A.M. the blockade-runner was discovered by the U.S.S. *Florida*, which began firing her twelve-pound howitzers.

With the pressure on, Captain Coxetter decided to beach the ship, hoping to save a portion of the cargo. As the crew headed for shore, one boat capsized and the captain and his paymaster were drowned. Some of the crew were captured by an armed cutter from the *Florida*.

The Unionists boarded the stranded blockade-runner and set her on fire. *Official Records* state that the *Fanny and Jenny* "burned all . . . night . . . completely destroyed by

---

* Marcus W. Price, "Ships That Tested The Blockade of the Carolina Ports, 1861–1865," *The American Neptune*, July 1948, p. 238.

fire." She exploded several times as her hold was full of gunpowder. In addition to the gunpowder, she was reported to have been carrying a quantity of gold and a gold presentation sword for General Robert E. Lee from British sympathizers.

For years the hulk of the *Fanny and Jenny* was visible at Wrightsville Beach. However, hurricane Hazel embedded her rusting hull more deeply in the sand in 1955. What is left of the ship today lies near the surf zone in the vicinity of the fishing pier.

The Yankees reported salvaging the vessel's C.S.A. flag, chronometer, sextant, and her navigational chart. Apparently, they overlooked the gold—and the jewel-studded sword. All records indicate that these invaluable relics are still there.

GEORGIANA C. McCAW
June 2, 1864
A Bloody Summer

The *McCaw* was a 700-ton side-wheel steamer out of Liverpool. Having left Nassau three days earlier, she was discovered early in the morning on June 2, 1864, as she raced for the entrance to Wilmington. Her cargo consisted of provisions and hardware for the Confederate Army. The blockade-runner was sighted by the U.S.S. *Victoria*, which began chase with a continuous round of fire.

Although the runner was within easy range of Fort Caswell, she struck the shoals of the western bar and settled in ten feet of water. Some provisions were salvaged before the ship was set on fire. Twenty-nine of the crew were captured as they headed for the beach. Union sailors boarded her and removed "two chronometers, one barometer, one sextant, and one marine clock." Two weeks after sinking, she was reported by the U.S.S. *State of Georgia* to be a complete wreck.

When the *McCaw* was beached, her pilot, Thomas Dyer, did not immediately strike out for shore as did the rest of the crew. He was reported to have had a quantity of gold aboard and stayed to secure it. A small boat later returned for him and, to the horror of its coxswain, pilot Dyer was found in a bloody heap with his skull crushed. The murderer was never arrested, nor was the money ever found. Whether the killer was a Yankee sailor or a traitor among the runner's crew, no one will ever know.

MARY BOWERS
August 30, 1864
"Damn the Torpedoes"

The *Mary Bowers*, a side-wheel steamer hailing from Glasgow, struck the wreck of the steamer *Georgiana* several miles east of Breach Inlet while maneuvering to enter Charleston Harbor. The ship was abandoned with the exception of a fourteen-year-old boy who was discovered by the Yankees the next day. The youngster stated that the runner had been commanded by a Scotsman named Hursey. It being only his second voyage, he panicked when the ship began sinking and ran for the boat, leaving the boy behind.

According to Captain De Camp of the U.S. Frigate *Wabash*, "The vessel is undoubtedly lying on the wreck of some vessel, as there is deep water all around her. Being almost entirely submerged, it is impossible to save anything from her. Her bell marked 1864, her binnacle and compasses, and two kedge anchors are saved; also a small quantity of liquor and a few signal flags."

The blockade-runner was a total loss. Her cargo was coal, and she sank about three quarters of a mile from shore off Long Island in three fathoms of water.

LYNX
September 25, 1864
Atlanta Has Fallen

The *Lynx* was a fast, two-masted, side-wheel steamer belonging to John Fraser and Company of Charleston. She was painted white, like many of the runners, to resemble clouds on a dark night. The ship had just been loaded with over 600 bales of cotton and also carried $50,000 in gold.

Lynx was outward bound for Bermuda and had crossed New Inlet Bar when she was sighted by three Union blockaders. The blockade-runner was extremely maneuverable, and she almost succeeded in running between the U.S. warships *Niphon*, *Buckingham*, and *Howquah*. But the *Howquah* caught the little vessel with two percussion shells from her thirty-pounder, one striking *Lynx*'s paddlebox and the other doing considerable damage forward. The runner finally was forced to slow down when *Niphon*'s broadsides found their mark. Seeing that she was cut off, the *Lynx* turned back toward shore and ran aground near Half Moon Battery, five miles above Fort Fisher. Her crew set the ship on fire and *Lynx* burned all night. She had been struck eight times, "six at or below the waterline." The *Wilmington Daily Journal* of October 3, 1864, reported that "Mr. Gordon, the purser, . . . had in charge fifty thousand dollars of government specie, and a large amount of bonds, both on government and private account. He saved these by his individual exertions, sacrificing his own interest to do so, losing everything he himself had on board, and getting to town with only the clothes he happened to have on his back."

CONSTANCE
October 5, 1864
Ships of the U.S. Navy Now Number Almost 700

No one knows how many trips the blockade-runner *Constance* made into the Confederacy. However, she carried a crew of twenty-nine and apparently was engaged in serious "trading" before being driven ashore and wrecked approximately one mile out and two miles East of Breach Inlet off Charleston. Charles W. Lee, acting master of the U.S.S. *Wamsutta*, reported on October 6, 1864: "I discovered a strange steamer sunk near the wrecks of the *Georgiana* and *Mary Bowers*. . . . I immediately went in a boat to examine her, but as she is completely submerged in about three fathoms of water I could ascertain nothing about her except that she is a Clyde-built vessel, of the class of the *Mary Bowers* and was evidently bound in.

"My opinion is that she struck the wreck of the *Georgiana* and put the wheel hard astarboard to clear it, thus bringing her head offshore and sinking so suddenly that she barely had time to take to her boats. She lies about 250 yards from and outside of the wrecks of the *Georgiana* and *Mary Bowers*. If divers could get to work on her before she breaks up, no doubt but that most of her cargo, if she has any, could be saved."

On October 8, 1864, another Union report confirmed the loss: "By an intercepted rebel dispatch we learn that the steamer discovered sunk on Long Island on the 6th instant was named the *Constance*. She is completely submerged, preventing the character of her cargo to be ascertained."

Constance was an 163-ton side-wheel steamer with two masts and two smokestacks.

FLORA
October 23, 1864
The Blockade Is Strangling the South

The blockade-runner *Flora* was considered an extremely profitable vessel, having made fourteen successful runs mostly between Charleston and Nassau. She carried a crew of thirty-nine, all of whom were experienced seamen. Most of her voyages were made under the name *Anna*. She was chased ashore while trying to enter Charleston Harbor. Confederate guns opened fire and struck her ninety-eight times after she stranded. This was done to prevent any Yankee salvage. J. Blakely Creighton, Commander of the U.S.S. *Mingoe*, said that "she passed us so quickly inshore that before I could slip or get my broadside to bear she was out of sight."

On October 24, 1864, William Ames, stationed on Morris Island, submitted the following report outlining the fate of the *Flora:*

"At daylight on October 23 a large side-wheel steamer, with two smokestacks, was discovered ashore opposite Battery Rutledge, Sullivan's Island, she having run on a shoal at that point during the night. This vessel was painted a lead color, was very long, and appeared to be of light draft. She is probably about 700 tons burden. The first shot fired at her was from the picket monitor; Fort Putnam opened at the same time with two 30-pounder Parrotts, striking her on the quarter at the second shot. Battery Chatfield opened with a 300-pounder Parrott; the third shell from this gun passed through the starboard wheelhouse into the vessel and exploded, tearing the wheel and wheelhouse all away and breaking up a large portion of her works amidships. Fort Strong opened with three 100-pounders, striking her many times in the hull and on her decks.

"The name of the vessel was the *Flora;* she was, no doubt,

running into Charleston at the time of getting aground. She now lies a complete wreck. This vessel was distant from Fort Putnam 2700 yards, from Battery Chatfield 2600 yards, and from Fort Strong 3500 yards."

STORMY PETREL
December 15, 1864
Sherman Has Burned Georgia

On October 23, 1864, the *Stormy Petrel* left Bermuda for Wilmington but failed to make port and returned to Bermuda. She left for Wilmington again on November 4, at that time commanded by a Captain Gordon. Sometime prior to the first of November her boilers had exploded at Bermuda, killing and wounding several (report of the *Wild Rover*). Upon arriving off New Inlet, the *Stormy Petrel* was unable to attain the safety of the inlet and was driven ashore by Union gunboats. She was reported by Colonel Lamb of Fort Fisher to have tried to come in "this morning but grounded well out on the south breakers." Power, Low and Company sent fifty Negroes to save the *Petrel*'s cargo. Finally, a northeast gale developed, leaving the *Stormy Petrel* a complete wreck. It is believed that two boatloads of cloth are all that were salvaged. She was known to be carrying a large cargo of arms and munitions of war, but little was saved because of inclement weather.

AGNES C. FREY
December 27, 1864
A Great Fleet Gathers Off Fort Fisher

This blockade-runner, also known as the *Fox*, was an extremely successful ship. She was reported to have made at least a dozen successful trips and possibly as many as seventeen before stranding two miles to the southward of Fort Caswell, four miles below the Western Bar.

The *Frey* was a steamer of about 350 tons. There are numerous references to her activities during 1864. Apparently, most of her runs were between Bermuda and Wilmington. She was, however, at Nassau in September of 1864. Little is known as to the causes of her loss, but it was ascertained that her pilot misjudged his position and ran upon the shoals below Fort Campbell while making his approach to the Cape Fear River. The estimated worth of the ship was $150,000. Her cargo at the time of sinking was unknown, but its loss was reported to have been of great consequence.

CELT
February 18, 1865
Charleston Is Evacuated

The blockade-running steamer *Celt* had made three previously successful runs and was on her fourth voyage from Charleston to Nassau loaded with cotton. Her captain knew that Charleston was being abandoned, so he determined to make a do-or-die dash for the sea. But the runner was forced ashore by Union gunboats while coming out of the channel. According to the report of Lieutenant-Commander Fillebrown, U.S.S. *Sonoma*, "The *Celt* lies stranded on the beach at Sullivan's Island back broken, full of water and decks ripped up. The machinery is in irreparable condition; some few pieces might be removed and be of service. Boilers are mostly below water, but judging from the condition of those parts visible, we are of the opinion they are not worth the expense of removing."

Official Records report that the *Celt* "had a valuable cargo of cotton, 190 bales of which was removed."

Bibliography

Abbott, John S. C., *The History of the Civil War in America*, New York, Henry Bill, 1866.

Alexander, E. P., *Military Memoirs of a Confederate;* a critical narrative, New York, Charles Scribner's Sons, 1907.

Almy, John J., *Incidents of the Blockade*, War Papers 9, Military Orders of Loyal Legion, Washington, 1892.

Avary, M. S., *A Virginia Girl in the Civil War 1861–1865*, New York, D. Appleton & Company, 1903.

Avirett, Rev. Jas. B., *The Memoirs of General Turner Ashby and His Compeers*, Baltimore, Selby & Dulany, 1867.

Battles and Leaders, New York, The Century Company, 1887.

Boatner, Mark Mayo, III, *The Civil War Dictionary*, New York, David McKay Co., Inc., 1959.

Boyd, Belle, *Belle Boyd in Camp and Prison*, New York, Blelock & Co., 1865.

Bradlee, Francis B. C., *Blockade Running During the Civil War*, Salem, Massachusetts, The Essex Institute, 1925.

Carse, Robert, *Blockade*, New York, Rinehart and Company, 1958.

Chestnut, Mary Boykin, *A Diary From Dixie*, New York, Appleton-Century-Crofts, 1905.

Cochran, Hamilton, *Blockade Runners of the Confederacy*, Indianapolis, Bobbs-Merrill Co., Inc., 1958.

Confederate Blockade Running Through Bermuda 1861–1865, edited by Frank E. Vandiver, Austin, University of Texas Press, 1947.

Cox, E. A. S. Mrs., *Memories of a South Carolina Plantation During the War*, in Charleston Library Society.

Davis, Jefferson, *The Rise and Fall of the Confederate Government*, Richmond, 1881.

Dawson, F. W., *Reminiscenses of Confederate Service*, Charleston, S.C., News and Courier Book Presses.

Dawson, S. M., *A Confederate Girl's Diary*, New York, Houghton, Mifflin Co., 1913.

DeLeon, T. C., *Four Years in Rebel Capitals:* an inside view of life in the Southern Confederacy, from birth to death, Mobile, Gossip Printing Co., 1890.

Douglas, H. K., *I Rode With Stonewall*, Chapel Hill, N.C. University of North Carolina Press, 1940.

Eggleston, G. C., *A Rebel's Recollections*, New York, G. Putnam & Sons, 1905.

Freeman, Douglas Southall, *Lee's Lieutenants*, New York, Charles Scribner's Sons, 1942.

Hill, Jim Dan, *Sea Dogs of the Sixties*, Minneapolis, The University of Minnesota Press, 1935.

Hopley, Catherine, *Life in the South During the War*, London, 1863.

Horner, Dave, *Key to Good Diving*, Virginia Beach, Virginia, Maritime Explorations, Ltd., 1963.

——*Shipwrecks, Skin Divers, and Sunken Gold*, New York, Dodd, Mead and Company, 1965.

——*Better Scuba Diving For Boys*, New York, Dodd, Mead and Company, 1966.

Howell, Andrew J., *The Book of Wilmington*.

Jervey, Theodore D., "Charleston During the Civil War." *Annual Report of the American Historical Association*, Washington, 1913.

Jones, J. B., *A Rebel War Clerk's Diary*, Philadelphia, J. B. Lippincott & Co., 1866.

Jones, Virgil Carrington, *The Civil War at Sea*, Holt, Rinehart, & Winston, 1960.

Maffitt, Emma Martin, *The Life and Services of John Newland Maffitt*, New York, The Neale Publishing Company, 1906.

Mahan, Alfred T., *The Navy in the Civil War*, New York, Charles Scribner's Sons, 1895.

Merrill, James M., *The Rebel Shore*, Boston, Little, Brown and Company 1957.

Molloy, Robert, *Charleston, A Gracious Heritage*, New York, D. Appleton-Century Co., Inc., 1947.

Morgan, James Morris, *Recollections of a Rebel Reefer*, Boston, Houghton, Mifflin and Company, 1917.

Newman, Ralph and E. B. Long, *The Civil War Digest*, New York, Grosset & Dunlap, 1956.

Official Records of the Union and Confederate Armies, Washington, U.S. Government Printing Office.

Official Records of the Union and Confederate Navies in the War of the Rebellion, Washington, U.S. Government Printing Office.

Pasha, Hobart, *Sketches From My Life,* New York, D. Appleton and Company, 1887.

Porter, Admiral David D., *The Naval History of the Civil War,* New York, The Sherman Publishing Company, 1886.

Price, Marcus W., "Ships That Tested the Blockade of the Carolina Ports, 1861–1865," *The American Neptune,* Vol. VIII, No. 8.

——"Ships That Tested the Blockade of the Gulf Ports, 1861–1865," *The American Neptune,* Vol. XI, No. 4.

——"Ships That Tested the Blockade of the Georgia and East Florida Ports, 1861–1865," *The American Neptune,* Vol. XV, No. 2.

Ross, Ishbel, *Rebel Rose,* New York, Harper & Brothers, 1954.

Scharf, J. Thomas, *History of the Confederate States Navy,* New York, Rogers and Sherwood, 1887.

Semmes, Raphael, *Service Afloat,* New York, P. J. Kenedy, 1903.

Siguad, Louis A., *Belle Boyd, Confederate Spy,* Richmond, The Dietz Press, 1944.

Simon, Katherine Drayton, *Stories of Charleston Harbor,* Columbia, S.C., The State Co., 1930.

Soley, James Russell, *The Blockade and the Cruisers,* New York, Charles Scribner's Sons, 1890.

Southern Historical Society, *Southern Historical Papers,* Richmond.

Sprunt, James, *Chronicles of the Cape Fear River,* Raleigh, N.C., Edwards and Broughton Company, 1914.

——*Derelicts,* Baltimore, The Lord Baltimore Press, 1920.

——*Running of the Blockade* (in Southern Historical Society Papers, Vol. 24).

Stern, Philip Van Doren, *The Confederate Navy, A Pictorial History,* New York, Doubleday and Co., Inc., 1962.

Stick, David, *Graveyard of the Atlantic,* Chapel Hill, The University of North Carolina Press, 1952.

Taylor, Thomas E., *Running the Blockade,* London, J. Murray, 1896.

The Official Atlas of the Civil War, New York, Thomas Yoseloff, 1958.

Watson, William, *The Adventures of a Blockade Runner,* New York, The Macmillan Company, 1892.

Wilkinson, John, *The Narrative of a Blockade Runner,* New York, Sheldon and Company, 1877.

Magazines,
Newspapers and Periodical Publications

Bermudian Magazine
Charleston Daily Courier
Charleston Mercury
Harpers Magazine
Illustrated London News
New York Herald
New York Times
New York Tribune
Norfolk Beacon
Norfolk Landmark
Norfolk Virginian-Pilot

Raleigh News and Observor
Richmond Times Dispatch
The Richmond Examiner
The Richmond Whig
The State Magazine
Washington National Intelligencer
Wilmington Daily Herald
Wilmington Daily Journal
Wilmington Messenger
Wilmington Morning Star

Index